VEGAN RUNNING

A COMPLETE GUIDE WITH 100 RUNNER WORKOUTS AND VEGAN MEAL PLANS

MARIANA CORREA

Copyright Page

2017 VEGAN RUNNING

ISBN - 9781979034036

All rights reserved. This book or any portion thereof may not be reproduced or used in any manner without the express written permission of the publisher except for the brief book quotations for reviews in the book. Scanning, uploading, and distributing of this book via the Internet or via any other means without the express permission of the publisher and author is illegal and punishable by law.
Only purchase authorized editions of this book. Please consult with your physician before training and using this book.

Acknowledgement

To my students, continue to challenge your mind and mind and you will be amazed with the results.

About the author

Mariana Correa is a certified professional coach and former professional tennis player. Mariana reached a career high of 26 in the world in juniors with wins over Anna Ivanovich (former #1 WTA in the world) and many other top 100 WTA players.

She competed successfully all over the world in over 26 countries and hundreds of cities including in London for Wimbledon, Paris for the French Open and in Australia for the world championships. She also represented Ecuador in Fed Cup, where the team reached the finals in their group.

During her career she was awarded the fair play award many times, proving to be not only an excellent player, but also a role model for other athletes.

Mariana is also a certified sports nutritionist with years of experience in proper nutrition and hydration for high performance athletes. She combines her love and knowledge in sports in this book to provide you with all the information you need to succeed.

Description

Are you looking to become faster, stronger, fitter and healthier? Perfect, **Vegan Running is exactly what you need to achieve your objectives.**

No boring explanations and useless context this book is exactly what you need to become the ultimate version of yourself.

100 Custom Runner Workouts each designed to:
- Improve your Endurance
- Increase your Speed and Pace
- Strengthen your Core
- Build Leg Explosiveness
- Burn Body Fat
- Achieve the Body you Always Dreamed of

Regardless of whether you are running for fun or training for a marathon, half marathon, 10k, 5k, you will improve your skills dramatically.

100 Days of Vegan Meal Plans will accompany each workout. Each day includes vegan breakfast, lunch, dinner and snacks each of these include a nutritional breakdown of how much fat, protein, carbohydrates, fiber and calories you will be consuming.

A vegan diet is ideal for those wishing to live a healthier lifestyle and boost their performance.

The author Mariana Correa is a former professional athlete and certified sports nutritionist that competed successfully all over the world. She shares years of experience both as an athlete and a coach bringing a priceless perspective.

Table of Contents

Acknowledgements

About the author

Description

Introduction: Runner's High

Chapter 1: Training for Success

Chapter 2: Nutrition is Everything

Introduction
Runner's High

Look at your running and your body capabilities at the present moment. Now imagine how you would like to be, what your goals are for your health, your running and your body.

A stronger, fitter and smarter version of you will always beat the current version of you, work hard these 2 months to become a better version of yourself.

The workouts in this book will challenge you to test your capabilities but if you commit to the program results will come.

Chapter 1:
Training for Success

Focus on working on the correct form on each exercise to get the maximum out of each exercise. Challenge your mind and your body even when you feel like you can't achieve your goal, keep training hard and every day you will be one step closer.

Feel free to adapt the workouts to push yourself harder or take it down a notch if you're not feeling well, the last thing you want is to get injured and have to miss a workout. Listen to your body, the key is to continue to work through every day to see the difference at the end of this 100 day awesome program.

Day 1   reps/sets

Strength training

Bench press	8/5
Push ups	12/8
Barbell bent over row	8/5
Pull ups	10/5
Lat pulldowns	10/4
Chin ups with bicep focus	10/3
Dips	15/5

Rest 25 seconds between sets, and 50 seconds between exercises, except on bench press and bent over rows, where you should rest 35 seconds between sets and 50 seconds between exercises. Use appropriate amount of weight on all exercises.

Day 2

Running

14 km with moderate speed break as necessary

Run 14 km continuously without taking a break.

Day 3
Strength training

Pistol squats	5 (Each leg)

Bodyweight squats 15

Tuck jumps	10

Standing one leg calf raises 10 (Each leg)

Repeat this cycle 4 times. Do not rest between exercises, and rest 1 minute and 30 seconds after each completed cycle.

Day 4

Running

500m as fast as you can/10

Run 500m as fast as you can. Rest 2 minutes after each completed km.

Day 5

Abs

Sit ups	15/4
Side plank	30 s (each side)
Hanging knee raises	10/4

Rest 10 seconds between sets and 35 seconds between exercises.

Day 6

Strength training

Back squats	8/5
Leg press	12/5
Standing calf raises	20/5
Box jumps	15/3

Perform box jumps as fast as you can. Do not lock your knees on leg press. Rest 25 seconds between sets and 50 seconds between exercises.

Day 7

Yoga day
1 hour of any kind of yoga training you would like. This will help you increase your flexibility and muscle recovery.

Day 8

Strength training

Exercise	Sets
Bench press	8/5
Push ups	15/6
Deadlift	5/5
Pull ups	12/4
Lat pulldowns	12/4
Chin ups with bicep focus	12/3
Dips	20/4

Rest 20 seconds between sets, and 40 seconds between exercises, except on bench press and deadlifts, where you should rest 35 seconds between sets and 50 seconds between exercises.

Day 9

Running

16 km with moderate speed

Run 16 km continuously without taking a break.

Day 10
Strength training

Pistol squats   8 (Each leg)

Bodyweight squats 15

Tuck jumps   12

Standing one leg calf raises 15 (Each leg)

Repeat this cycle 4 times. Do not rest between exercises, and rest 1 minute and 30 seconds after each completed cycle.

Day 11

Running

Endurance

500m as fast as you can/12

Run 500m as fast as you can. Rest 2 minutes after each completed 500m.

Day 12

Abs

Sit ups	20/3
Side plank	45 s (each side)
Hanging knee raises	10/5
Plank	30s

Rest 10 seconds between sets and 30 seconds between exercises.

Day 13

Strength training

Back squats   5/5 +2.5kg or 10/5

Leg press   15/4

Standing calf raises 25/4

Box jumps   15/4

Add 2.5 kg to your back squat. If you can't perform most of the reps with proper form, go heavier on your next workout. Perform box jumps as fast as you can. Do not lock your knees on leg press. Rest 25 seconds between sets and 50 seconds between exercises.

Day 14

Flexibility Day

Use this day to recover from your workouts. You will warm up lightly with a 5 minute jog and proceed to stretch every muscle in your body. Hold each stretch for 30 seconds and repeat each stretch 3 times. Try to increase your flexibility with each stretch.

Day 15

Strength training

Exercise	Sets
Bench press	8/5
Push ups	20/5
Deadlift	10/5
Pull ups	12/5
Lat pulldowns	15/4
Chin ups with bicep focus	12/4
Dips	20/5

Rest 20 seconds between sets, and 40 seconds between exercises, except on bench press and deadlifts, where you should rest 35 seconds between sets and 50 seconds between exercises.

Day 16

Running

18 km with moderate speed

Run 18 km continuously without taking a break.

Day 17

Strength training

Pistol squats 10 (Each leg)

Bodyweight squats 20

Tuck jumps 12

Standing one leg calf raises 15 (Each leg)

Repeat this cycle 4 times. Do not rest between exercises, and rest 1 minute and 30 seconds after each completed cycle.

Day 18

Endurance

500m as fast as you can/14

Run 500m as fast as you can. Rest 2 minutes after each completed 500m.

Day 19

Abs

Sit ups	20/4
Side plank	1 minute (each side)
Hanging knee raises	12/5
Plank	45s

Rest 10 seconds between sets and 30 seconds between exercises.

Day 20
Strength training

Back squats   5/5 +2.5kg or 10/5

Leg press   15/4

Standing calf raises 15/5 +5kg or 25/5

Box jumps   20/4

Add 2.5 kg to your back squat and 5kg to your standing calf raises. If you can't perform most of the reps with proper form, go heavier on your next workout. Perform box jumps as fast as you can. Do not lock your knees on leg press. Rest 25 seconds between sets and 50 seconds between exercises.

Day 21

Active Recovery Day

This day will be used to recover your body and muscles. You will warm up with some light cardio, and stretch all the muscles in your body. Followed by a massage, foam roller or a very hot bath/jacuzzi to relax the muscle tissues.

Day 22

Strength training

Bench press 5/5 +2.5kg or 10/5

Push ups 25/4

Deadlift 5/5 +2.5kg or 10/6

Pull ups 15/4

Lat pulldowns 15/5

Chin ups with bicep focus 12/5

Dips 25/4

Add 2.5 kg to your bench press and deadlift. If you can't perform most of the reps with proper form, increase the weight on your next workout. Rest 20 seconds between sets, and 40 seconds between exercises, except on bench press and deadlifts, where you should rest 35 seconds between sets and 50 seconds between. Use appropriate amount of weight on all exercises.

Day 23

Running

20 km with moderate speed

Run 20 km continuously without taking a break.

Day 24

Strength training

Pistol squats   12 (Each leg)

Bodyweight squats 20

Tuck jumps   15

Standing one leg calf raises 20 (Each leg)

Repeat this cycle 4 times. Do not rest between exercises, and rest 1 minute and 45 seconds after each completed cycle.

Day 25

Endurance

500m as fast as you can/16

Run 500m as fast as you can. Rest 2 minutes after each completed 500m.

Day 26

Abs

Sit ups 20/5
Side plank 1 minute,15 seconds(each side)
Hanging knee raises 15/4
Plank 1 minute

Rest 10 seconds between sets and 30 seconds between exercises.

Day 27
Strength training

Back squats   8/5

Leg press   15/5

Standing calf raises 20/4

Box jumps   20/5

Perform box jumps as fast as you can. Do not lock your knees on leg press. Rest 25 seconds between sets and 50 seconds between exercises.

Day 28

Flexibility Day

Use this day to recover from your workouts. You will warm up lightly with a 5 minute jog and proceed to stretch every muscle in your body. Hold each stretch for 30 seconds and repeat each stretch 3 times. Try to increase your flexibility with each stretch.

Day 29

Strength training

Exercise	Sets/Reps
Bench press	8/5
Push ups	25/5
Deadlift	8/5
Pull ups	15/5
Lat pulldowns	10/5 +5kg or 20/5
Chin ups with bicep focus	15/4
Dips	25/5

Add 5 kg to your lat pulldown. If you can't perform most of the reps with proper form, increase the weight on your next workout. Rest 20 seconds between sets, and 40 seconds between exercises, except on bench press and deadlifts, where you should rest 35 seconds between sets and 50 seconds between. Use appropriate amount of weight on all exercises.

Day 30

Running

20 km with moderate speed

Run 20 km continuously without taking a break.

Day 31
Strength training

Pistol squats   14(Each leg)

Bodyweight squats 20

Tuck jumps   20

Standing one leg calf raises 22 (Each leg)

Repeat this cycle 4 times. Do not rest between exercises, and rest 2 minutes after each completed cycle.

Day 32

Endurance

500m as fast as you can/18

Run 500m as fast as you can. Rest 2 minutes after each completed 500m.

Day 33

Abs

Sit ups 25/4
Side plank 1 minute, 30 seconds (each side)
Hanging knee raises 20/3
Plank 1 minute and 15 seconds

Rest 10 seconds between sets and 30 seconds between exercises.

Day 34

Strength training

Back squats   10/5

Leg press   10/5 +5kg or 20/4

Standing calf raises 25/4

Box jumps   25/4

Add 5kg to your leg press. If you can't perform most of the reps with proper form, increase the weight on your next workout. Perform box jumps as fast as you can. Do not lock your knees on leg press. Rest 25 seconds between sets and 50 seconds between exercises.

Day 35

Yoga day
1 hour of any kind of yoga training you would like. This will help you increase your flexibility and muscle recovery.

Day 36
Strength training

Exercise	Sets/Reps
Bench press	10/5
Push ups	30/4
Deadlift	5/5 +2.5kg or 10/5
Pull ups	15/5
Lat pulldowns	12/5
Chin ups with bicep focus	18/3
Dips	30/4

Add 2.5 kg to your deadlift. If you can't perform most of the reps with proper form, increase the weight on your next workout. Rest 30 seconds between sets, and 40 seconds between exercises, except on bench press and deadlifts, where you should rest 40 seconds between sets and 1 minute between exercises. Use appropriate amount of weight on all exercises.

Day 37

Running

22 km with moderate speed

Run 22 km continuously without taking a break.

Day 38

Strength training

Pistol squats 14 (Each leg)

Bodyweight squats 25

Tuck jumps 20

Standing one leg calf raises 25 (Each leg)

Repeat this cycle 4 times. Do not rest between exercises, and rest 2 minutes after each completed cycle.

Day 39

Endurance

500m as fast as you can/20

Run 500m as fast as you can. Rest 2 minutes after each completed 500m.

Day 40

Abs

Sit ups 25/5
Side plank 1 minute, 45 seconds (each side)
Hanging leg raises 10/4
Plank 1 minute and 30 seconds

Rest 10 seconds between sets and 30 seconds between exercises.

Day 41

Strength training

Back squats   5/5 +2.5kg, or 10/6

Leg press   10/6

Standing calf raises 15/5 +5kg or 25/5

Box jumps   30/4

Add 2.5kg to your back squat, and 5kg to your standing calf raise. If you can't perform most of the reps with proper form, increase the weight on your next workout. Perform box jumps as fast as you can. Do not lock your knees on leg press. Rest 25 seconds between sets and 50 seconds between exercises.

Day 42

Active Recovery day

This day will be used to recover your body and muscles. You will warm up with some light cardio, and stretch all the muscles in your body. Followed by a massage, foam roller or a very hot bath/jacuzzi to relax the muscle tissues.

Day 43

Strength training
Bench press 5/5 +2.5kg or 10/6

Exercise	Reps/Sets
Push ups	30/5
Deadlift	8/5
Pull ups	20/4
Lat pulldowns	15/4
Chin ups with bicep focus	20/3
Dips	30/5

Add 2.5 kg to your deadlift. If you can't perform most of the reps with proper form, increase the weight on your next workout. Rest 35 seconds between sets, and 50 seconds between exercises, except on bench press and deadlifts, where you should rest 45 seconds between sets and 1 minute and 15 seconds between exercises. Use appropriate amount of weight on all exercises.

Day 44

Running

24 km with moderate speed

Run 24 km continuously without taking a break.

Day 45

Strength training

Pistol squats 16(Each leg)

Bodyweight squats 30

Tuck jumps 20

Standing one leg calf raises 30 (Each leg)

Repeat this cycle 4 times. Do not rest between exercises, and rest 2 minutes after each completed cycle.

Day 46

Endurance

500m as fast as you can/23

Run 500m as fast as you can. Rest 2 minutes after each completed 500m.

Day 47

Abs

Sit ups 30/4
Side plank 2 minutes (each side)
Hanging leg raises 10/5
Plank 1 minute and 45 seconds

Rest 15 seconds between sets and 45 seconds between exercises.

Day 48

Strength training

Back squats   8/5

Leg press   15/4

Standing calf raises 20/4

Box jumps   30/4

Perform box jumps as fast as you can. Do not lock your knees on leg press. Rest 25 seconds between sets and 50 seconds between exercises.

Day 49

Flexibility Day

Use this day to recover from your workouts. You will warm up lightly with a 5 minute jog and proceed to stretch every muscle in your body. Hold each stretch for 30 seconds and repeat each stretch 3 times. Try to increase your flexibility with each stretch.

Day 50

Strength training

Exercise	Sets/Reps
Bench press	8/5
Push ups	35/4
Deadlift	10/5
Pull ups	20/5
Lat pulldowns	10/4 +5kg, or 20/4
Chin ups with bicep focus	20/4
Dips	35/4

Add 5 kg to your lat pulldowns. If you can't perform most of the reps with proper form, increase the weight on your next workout. Rest 45 seconds between sets, and 1 minute between exercises, except on bench press and deadlifts, where you should rest 45 seconds between sets and 1 minute and 30 seconds between exercises. Use appropriate amount of weight on all exercises.

Day 51

Running

26 km with moderate speed

Run 26 km continuously without taking a break.

Day 52

Strength training

Pistol squats 18 (Each leg)

Bodyweight squats 30

Tuck jumps 25

Standing one leg calf raises 35 (Each leg)

Repeat this cycle 4 times. Do not rest between exercises, and rest 2 minutes after each completed cycle.

Day 53

Endurance

500m as fast as you can/25

Run 500m as fast as you can. Rest 2 minutes after each completed 500m.

Day 54

Abs

Sit ups	30/5
Side plank 2 minutes (each side)	
Hanging leg raises	15/4
Plank	2 minutes

Rest 20 seconds between sets and 45 seconds between exercises.

Day 55

Strength training

Back squats   10/5

Leg press   15/4

Standing calf raises 20/5

Box jumps   30/5

Perform box jumps as fast as you can. Do not lock your knees on leg press. Rest 30 seconds between sets and 1 minute between exercises.

Day 56

Active Recovery Day

This day will be used to recover your body and muscles. You will warm up with some light cardio, and stretch all the muscles in your body. Followed by a massage, foam roller or a very hot bath/jacuzzi to relax the muscle tissues.

Day 57

Running

28 km with moderate speed

Run 28 km continuously without taking a break.

Day 58

Abs

Sit ups	35/4
Side plank	2 minutes (each side)
Hanging leg raises	15/5
Plank	2 minutes

Rest 20 seconds between sets and 45 seconds between exercises.

Day 59

Pistol squats 20 (Each leg)

Bodyweight squats 35

Tuck jumps 25

Standing one leg calf raises 40 (Each leg)

Repeat this cycle 4 times. Do not rest between exercises, and rest 2 minutes after each completed cycle.

Day 60

Yoga/ Flexibility Day

Use this day to recover from your workouts. You will warm up lightly with a 5 minute jog and proceed to stretch every muscle in your body. Hold each stretch for 30 seconds and repeat each stretch 3 times. Try to increase your flexibility with each stretch.

Or

1 hour of any kind of yoga training you would like. This will help you increase your flexibility and muscle recovery.

Day 61

Strength training

Exercise	Sets
Bench press	8/5
Push ups	15/6
Deadlift	5/5
Pull ups	12/4
Lat pulldowns	12/4
Chin ups with bicep focus	12/3
Dips	20/4

Rest 20 seconds between sets, and 40 seconds between exercises, except on bench press and deadlifts, where you should rest 35 seconds between sets and 50 seconds between exercises.

Day 62

Running

16 km with moderate speed

Run 16 km continuously without taking a break.

Day 63
Strength training

Pistol squats 8 (Each leg)

Bodyweight squats 15

Tuck jumps 12

Standing one leg calf raises 15 (Each leg)

Repeat this cycle 4 times. Do not rest between exercises, and rest 1 minute and 30 seconds after each completed cycle.

Day 64

Running

Endurance

500m as fast as you can/12

Run 500m as fast as you can. Rest 2 minutes after each completed 500m.

Day 65

Abs

Sit ups	20/3
Side plank	45 s (each side)
Hanging knee raises	10/5
Plank	30s

Rest 10 seconds between sets and 30 seconds between exercises.

Day 66

Strength training

Back squats 5/5 +2.5kg or 10/5

Leg press 15/4

Standing calf raises 25/4

Box jumps 15/4

Add 2.5 kg to your back squat. If you can't perform most of the reps with proper form, go heavier on your next workout. Perform box jumps as fast as you can. Do not lock your knees on leg press. Rest 25 seconds between sets and 50 seconds between exercises.

Day 67

Flexibility Day

Use this day to recover from your workouts. You will warm up lightly with a 5 minute jog and proceed to stretch every muscle in your body. Hold each stretch for 30 seconds and repeat each stretch 3 times. Try to increase your flexibility with each stretch.

Day 68

Strength training

Bench press 5/5 +2.5kg or 10/5

Push ups — 25/4

Deadlift — 5/5 +2.5kg or 10/6

Pull ups — 15/4

Lat pulldowns — 15/5

Chin ups with bicep focus 12/5

Dips — 25/4

Add 2.5 kg to your bench press and deadlift. If you can't perform most of the reps with proper form, increase the weight on your next workout. Rest 20 seconds between sets, and 40 seconds between exercises, except on bench press and deadlifts, where you should rest 35 seconds between sets and 50 seconds between. Use appropriate amount of weight on all exercises.

Day 69

Running

20 km with moderate speed

Run 20 km continuously without taking a break.

Day 70

Strength training

Pistol squats 12 (Each leg)

Bodyweight squats 20

Tuck jumps 15

Standing one leg calf raises 20 (Each leg)

Repeat this cycle 4 times. Do not rest between exercises, and rest 1 minute and 45 seconds after each completed cycle.

Day 71

Endurance

500m as fast as you can/16

Run 500m as fast as you can. Rest 2 minutes after each completed 500m.

Day 72

Abs

Sit ups 20/5
Side plank 1 minute,15 seconds(each side)
Hanging knee raises 15/4
Plank 1 minute

Rest 10 seconds between sets and 30 seconds between exercises.

Day 73
Strength training

Back squats   8/5

Leg press   15/5

Standing calf raises 20/4

Box jumps   20/5

Perform box jumps as fast as you can. Do not lock your knees on leg press. Rest 25 seconds between sets and 50 seconds between exercises.

Day 74

Flexibility Day

Use this day to recover from your workouts. You will warm up lightly with a 5 minute jog and proceed to stretch every muscle in your body. Hold each stretch for 30 seconds and repeat each stretch 3 times. Try to increase your flexibility with each stretch.

Day 75

Strength training

Exercise	Reps/Sets
Bench press	8/5
Push ups	25/5
Deadlift	8/5
Pull ups	15/5
Lat pulldowns	10/5 +5kg or 20/5
Chin ups with bicep focus	15/4
Dips	25/5

Add 5 kg to your lat pulldown. If you can't perform most of the reps with proper form, increase the weight on your next workout. Rest 20 seconds between sets, and 40 seconds between exercises, except on bench press and deadlifts, where you should rest 35 seconds between sets and 50 seconds between. Use appropriate amount of weight on all exercises.

Day 76

Running

20 km with moderate speed

Run 20 km continuously without taking a break.

Day 77
Strength training

Pistol squats   14(Each leg)

Bodyweight squats 20

Tuck jumps   20

Standing one leg calf raises 22 (Each leg)

Repeat this cycle 4 times. Do not rest between exercises, and rest 2 minutes after each completed cycle.

Day 78

Endurance

500m as fast as you can/18

Run 500m as fast as you can. Rest 2 minutes after each completed 500m.

Day 79

Abs

Sit ups 25/4
Side plank 1 minute, 30 seconds (each side)
Hanging knee raises 20/3
Plank 1 minute and 15 seconds

Rest 10 seconds between sets and 30 seconds between exercises.

Day 80

Strength training

Back squats   10/5

Leg press   10/5 +5kg or 20/4

Standing calf raises 25/4

Box jumps   25/4

Add 5kg to your leg press. If you can't perform most of the reps with proper form, increase the weight on your next workout. Perform box jumps as fast as you can. Do not lock your knees on leg press. Rest 25 seconds between sets and 50 seconds between exercises.

Day 81

Yoga day
1 hour of any kind of yoga training you would like. This will help you increase your flexibility and muscle recovery.

Day 82

Strength training
Bench press 5/5 +2.5kg or 10/6

Exercise	Sets/Reps
Push ups	30/5
Deadlift	8/5
Pull ups	20/4
Lat pulldowns	15/4
Chin ups with bicep focus	20/3
Dips	30/5

Add 2.5 kg to your deadlift. If you can't perform most of the reps with proper form, increase the weight on your next workout. Rest 35 seconds between sets, and 50 seconds between exercises, except on bench press and deadlifts, where you should rest 45 seconds between sets and 1 minute and 15 seconds between exercises. Use appropriate amount of weight on all exercises.

Day 83

Running

24 km with moderate speed

Run 24 km continuously without taking a break.

Day 84

Strength training

Pistol squats   16(Each leg)

Bodyweight squats 30

Tuck jumps   20

Standing one leg calf raises 30 (Each leg)

Repeat this cycle 4 times. Do not rest between exercises, and rest 2 minutes after each completed cycle.

Day 85

Endurance

500m as fast as you can/23

Run 500m as fast as you can. Rest 2 minutes after each completed 500m.

Day 86

Abs

Sit ups 30/4
Side plank 2 minutes (each side)
Hanging leg raises 10/5
Plank 1 minute and 45 seconds

Rest 15 seconds between sets and 45 seconds between exercises.

Day 87

Strength training

Back squats   8/5

Leg press   15/4

Standing calf raises 20/4

Box jumps   30/4

Perform box jumps as fast as you can. Do not lock your knees on leg press. Rest 25 seconds between sets and 50 seconds between exercises.

Day 88

Flexibility Day

Use this day to recover from your workouts. You will warm up lightly with a 5 minute jog and proceed to stretch every muscle in your body. Hold each stretch for 30 seconds and repeat each stretch 3 times. Try to increase your flexibility with each stretch.

Day 89

Strength training

Exercise	Sets/Reps
Bench press	8/5
Push ups	35/4
Deadlift	10/5
Pull ups	20/5
Lat pulldowns	10/4 +5kg, or 20/4
Chin ups with bicep focus	20/4
Dips	35/4

Add 5 kg to your lat pulldowns. If you can't perform most of the reps with proper form, increase the weight on your next workout. Rest 45 seconds between sets, and 1 minute between exercises, except on bench press and deadlifts, where you should rest 45 seconds between sets and 1 minute and 30 seconds between exercises. Use appropriate amount of weight on all exercises.

Day 90

Running

26 km with moderate speed

Run 26 km continuously without taking a break.

Day 91

Strength training

Pistol squats 18 (Each leg)

Bodyweight squats 30

Tuck jumps 25

Standing one leg calf raises 35 (Each leg)

Repeat this cycle 4 times. Do not rest between exercises, and rest 2 minutes after each completed cycle.

Day 92

Endurance

500m as fast as you can/25

Run 500m as fast as you can. Rest 2 minutes after each completed 500m.

Day 93

Abs

Sit ups	30/5
Side plank	2 minutes (each side)
Hanging leg raises	15/4
Plank	2 minutes

Rest 20 seconds between sets and 45 seconds between exercises.

Day 94

Strength training

Back squats	10/5

Leg press	15/4

Standing calf raises 20/5

Box jumps	30/5

Perform box jumps as fast as you can. Do not lock your knees on leg press. Rest 30 seconds between sets and 1 minute between exercises.

Day 95

Active Recovery Day

This day will be used to recover your body and muscles. You will warm up with some light cardio, and stretch all the muscles in your body. Followed by a massage, foam roller or a very hot bath/jacuzzi to relax the muscle tissues.

Day 96

Running

28 km with moderate speed

Run 28 km continuously without taking a break.

Day 97

Abs

Sit ups	35/4
Side plank	2 minutes (each side)
Hanging leg raises	15/5
Plank	2 minutes

Rest 20 seconds between sets and 45 seconds between exercises.

Day 98

Pistol squats   20 (Each leg)

Bodyweight squats 35

Tuck jumps   25

Standing one leg calf raises 40 (Each leg)

Repeat this cycle 4 times. Do not rest between exercises, and rest 2 minutes after each completed cycle.

Day 99

Running

24 km with moderate speed

Day 100

Yoga/ Flexibility Day

Use this day to recover from your workouts. You will warm up lightly with a 5 minute jog and proceed to stretch every muscle in your body. Hold each stretch for 30 seconds and repeat each stretch 3 times. Try to increase your flexibility with each stretch.

Or

1 hour of any kind of yoga training you would like. This will help you increase your flexibility and muscle recovery.

Chapter 2:
Nutrition is Everything

Feeding your body properly is crucial to performing at a top level. Your body runs on whatever you feed it. Your meals are your fuel. If you want your body to perform at its full potential, you must keep it perfectly fine tuned.

Each day you will find a right balance of protein, carbs, fiber and fat to keep your body at optimal levels. I would like to suggest you modify this plan according to your own weight, age, health condition and workouts as well. Choose your meals according to what time of day you will be training. For example, before a workout you would need more energy so you would choose a meal which would contain more carbohydrates. After a workout you would need to replenish your body so I would suggest either a snack or a meal with a greater amount of protein.

If a certain ingredient mentioned in a daily meal is not in season or not available near you, you may choose another healthy and nutritious alternative. The main goal is to fuel your body in the best way possible so it can help you achieve your dreams.

Day 1
Breakfast:
½ cup rolled oats
1 tbsp flaxseed
½ cup coconut milk
Nutritional values: Kcal: 468 Protein: 9.4g, Carbs: 36.4g, Dietary Fiber: 8.7g, Fats: 33.5g

Snack:
1 oz pecans
1 large orange
Nutritional values: Kcal: 284 Protein: 4.8g, Carbs: 25.7g, Dietary Fiber: 7.5g, Fats: 4.8g

Lunch:
1 large zucchini, grilled and seasoned with 1 tbsp olive oil
2 slices buckwheat bread
1 pear
Nutritional values: Kcal: 403 Protein: 8.7g, Carbs: 60.7g, Dietary Fiber: 9.2g, Fats: 16.6g

Snack:
3 cups pineapple chunks, juiced
1 large apple, juiced
Nutritional values: Kcal: 315 Protein: 3.5g, Carbs: 92g, Dietary Fiber: 12.7g, Fats: 0.9g

Dinner
10 oz mushrooms, grilled
½ cup basmati rice, cooked
Nutritional values: Kcal: 398 Protein: 15.5g, Carbs: 83.3g, Dietary Fiber: 4g, Fats: 1.4g

Day2
Breakfast:
1 cup almond yogurt
1 tbsp chia seeds
3 figs
1 cup of black coffee
Nutritional values: Kcal: 457 Protein: 22.1g, Carbs: 64.2g, Dietary Fiber: 16g, Fats: 13.1g
Snack:
½ avocado, grilled
3 plums
Nutritional values: Kcal: 295 Protein: 3.4g, Carbs: 32.6g, Dietary Fiber: 9.4g, Fats: 20.2g
Lunch:
1 cup green peas, cooked
½ cup hummus
7 oz mushrooms, grilled
1.5 oz cauliflower, grilled
Nutritional values: Kcal: 392 Protein: 25.9g, Carbs: 50.6g, Dietary Fiber: 19.4g, Fats: 13.2g
Snack:
1 large apple
2 medium-sized carrots
2 oz prunes
Nutritional values: Kcal: 302 Protein: 2.8g, Carbs: 79g, Dietary Fiber: 12.4g, Fats: 0.6g
Dinner:
7 oz buckwheat noodles, cooked and seasoned with one tablespoon of olive oil
2 oz spring onions, steamed
Nutritional values: Kcal: 412 Protein: 10.1g, Carbs: 54.1g, Dietary Fiber: 3.8g, Fats: 18.2g

Day 3
Breakfast:
10 oz tomatoes, grilled
7 oz asparagus, grilled
1 cup of freshly squeezed orange juice
4 large figs
Nutritional values: Kcal: 392 Protein: 11.1g, Carbs: 93.1g, Dietary Fiber: 15.5g, Fats: 2g
Snack:
1 cup grapes
1 large mango
2 kiwis
Nutritional values: Kcal: 355 Protein: 5.1g, Carbs: 88.1g, Dietary Fiber: 10.4g, Fats: 2.4g
Lunch:
7 oz artichoke
½ cup kidney beans
1 tbsp extra virgin olive oil
Nutritional values: Kcal: 523 Protein: 27.2g, Carbs: 77.2g, Dietary Fiber: 24.7g, Fats: 15.3g
Snack:
1 large apple
Nutritional values: Kcal: 116 Protein: 0.6g, Carbs: 30.8g, Dietary Fiber: 5.4g, Fats: 0.4g
Dinner:
7 oz arugula
1 cup raspberries
1 oz walnuts
1 cup freshly squeezed orange juice
Nutritional values: Kcal: 401 Protein: 15.1g, Carbs: 50.5g, Dietary Fiber: 13.6g, Fats: 19.3g

Day 4
Breakfast:
2 bananas
1 tbsp pure coconut nectar
1 tbsp flaxseed
1 cup freshly squeezed lemonade
Nutritional values: Kcal: 369 Protein: 5.9g, Carbs: 78.3g, Dietary Fiber: 9.1g, Fats: 4.9g

Snack:
½ cup blueberries
1 oz almonds, toasted
1 oz walnuts
Nutritional values: Kcal: 381 Protein: 13.4g, Carbs: 19.4g, Dietary Fiber: 7.2g, Fats: 31.2g

Lunch:
3 oz red lentils, cooked
1 carrot cooked
7 oz kale, steamed
2 oz lettuce
Nutritional values: Kcal: 435 Protein: 28.7g, Carbs: 80.6g, Dietary Fiber: 31g, Fats: 1g

Snack:
3 cups honeydew melon, juiced
1 cup watermelon, diced
Nutritional values: Kcal: 203 Protein: 3.5g, Carbs: 55g, Dietary Fiber: 4.5g, Fats: 0.9g

Dinner:
5 oz eggplant, steamed
½ cup red lentils, cooked
2 cherry tomatoes, fresh
Nutritional values: Kcal: 419 Protein: 28.3g, Carbs: 75.6g, Dietary Fiber: 37.2g, Fats: 1.8g

Day 5:
Breakfast:
½ cup quinoa, cooked
3 tbsp raisins
¼ cup coconut milk
1 cup of black coffee
Nutritional values: Kcal: 532 Protein: 14.2g, Carbs: 79.4g, Dietary Fiber: 8.3g, Fats: 19.6g
Snack:
1 oz pecan nuts
Nutritional values: Kcal: 197 Protein: 3g, Carbs: 4g, Dietary Fiber: 3g, Fats: 20.2g
Lunch:
2 medium-sized corn tortillas
¼ cup black beans, cooked
1 large tomato, diced
7 oz of spinach, steamed
1 red bell pepper
Nutritional values: Kcal: 386 Protein: 21.7g, Carbs: 75g, Dietary Fiber: 18.5g, Fats: 3.5g
Snack:
1 cup cantaloupe
6 dates
Nutritional values: Kcal: 193 Protein: 2.5g, Carbs: 50.1g, Dietary Fiber: 5.4g, Fats: 0.5g
Dinner:
1 cup edamame hummus
½ cup beets, cooked
½ cup shallots, fresh
Nutritional values: Kcal: 471 Protein: 36.6g, Carbs: 50.2g, Dietary Fiber: 12.4g, Fats: 17.6g

Day 6:
Breakfast:
1 cup of strawberries, fresh
½ cup raspberries, fresh
5 almonds, toasted
½ cup almond yogurt
1 cup of herbal tea
Nutritional values: Kcal: 200 Protein: 10g, Carbs: 28.3g, Dietary Fiber: 7.6g, Fats: 5.3g

Snack:
1 peach
2 oz pecan nuts
Nutritional values: Kcal: 454 Protein: 7.5g, Carbs: 22.1g, Dietary Fiber: 8.4g, Fats: 40.9g

Lunch:
4 Roma tomatoes, grilled
½ cup rice, cooked
½ spinach, steamed
Nutritional values: Kcal: 436 Protein: 11.9g, Carbs: 92g, Dietary Fiber: 9.5g, Fats: 3.6g

Snack:
1 red bell pepper
1 yellow bell pepper
1 green bell pepper
1 cup avocado chunks
Nutritional values: Kcal: 412 Protein: 6.4g, Carbs: 39.6g, Dietary Fiber: 14.6g, Fats: 29.4g

Dinner:
3.5 oz buckwheat pasta, cooked
1 large tomato
3.5 oz lettuce
Nutritional values: Kcal: 330 Protein: 13.2g, Carbs: 63.9g, Dietary Fiber: 2.7g, Fats: 2.8g

Day 7:
Breakfast:
2 large oranges, broiled
2 oz walnuts
1 cup of herbal tea
Nutritional values: Kcal: 523 Protein: 17.1g, Carbs: 48.9g, Dietary Fiber: 12.7g, Fats: 33.9g

Snack:
4 medium-sized oranges, juiced
Nutritional values: Kcal: 200 Protein: 4.9g, Carbs: 64.5g, Dietary Fiber: 12.4g, Fats: 0.6g

Lunch:
2 cup butternut squash, cooked
1 cup Brussel sprouts, cooked
1 cup leeks, cooked
1 tbsp olive oil
Nutritional values: Kcal: 338 Protein: 71g, Carbs: 53.3g, Dietary Fiber: 10.5g, Fats: 14.8g

Snack:
7 oz chestnuts, baked
Nutritional values: Kcal: 389 Protein: 3.2g, Carbs: 87.7g, Dietary Fiber: 8.7g, Fats: 2.5g

Dinner:
5 oz orzo pasta, cooked
½ cup zucchini, grilled
Nutritional values: Kcal: 417 Protein: 16.7g, Carbs: 79.5g, Dietary Fiber: 0.6g, Fats: 3.4g

Day 8:
Breakfast:
10 oz grilled red peppers
10 oz melon
4 pecans
1 cup of herbal tea
Nutritional values: Kcal: 212 Protein: 7.7g, Carbs: 48.6g, Dietary Fiber: 6.8g, Fats: 1.8g
Snack:
1 oz pecan nuts
Nutritional values: Kcal: 395 Protein: 6.1g, Carbs: 8.1g, Dietary Fiber: 6.1g, Fats: 40.5g
Lunch:
5 oz mushrooms, grilled
1 white onion, grilled
1 tbsp olive oil
Nutritional values: Kcal: 241 Protein: 3.4g, Carbs: 29.8g, Dietary Fiber: 5.3g, Fats: 14.4g
Snack:
7 oz avocado, baked
Nutritional values: Kcal: 405 Protein: 3.8g, Carbs: 17.1g, Dietary Fiber: 13.3g, Fats: 38.7g
Dinner:
1 tomato, fire-roasted
1 zucchini, grilled
7 oz turnip greens, fresh
1 oz walnuts
1 cup freshly squeezed orange juice
Nutritional values: Kcal: 393 Protein: 14.4g, Carbs: 51.7g, Dietary Fiber: 11.7g, Fats: 18.3g

Day 9:
Breakfast:
10 oz grilled red peppers
2 oz quinoa, cooked
10 oz melon
4 pecans
1 cup of herbal tea
Nutritional values: Kcal: 421 Protein: 15.7g, Carbs: 85g, Dietary Fiber: 10.8g, Fats: 5.2g
Snack:
1 kiwi
1.5 oz almonds, toasted
Nutritional values: Kcal: 292 Protein: 9.9g, Carbs: 20.2g, Dietary Fiber: 7.6g, Fats: 21.7g
Lunch:
5 oz arugula, fresh
½ cup white beans, cooked
1 red onion, fresh
Nutritional values: Kcal: 416 Protein: 28.5g, Carbs: 76.3g, Dietary Fiber: 20g, Fats: 1.9g
Snack:
1 medium apple
1 banana
Nutritional values: Kcal: 221 Protein: 1.9g, Carbs: 57.8g, Dietary Fiber: 8.5g, Fats: 0.8g
Dinner:
3.5 oz buckwheat noodles, cooked and seasoned with one tablespoon of olive oil
2 oz spring onions, steamed
3.5 oz kale, steamed
Nutritional values: Kcal: 512 Protein: 16.1g, Carbs: 83.1g, Dietary Fiber: 12.7g, Fats: 17.2g

Day 10
Breakfast:
¼ cup rolled oats
¼ cup almond milk
5 oz cherries
Nutritional values: Kcal: 379 Protein: 4.6g, Carbs: 56.8g, Dietary Fiber: 4.2g, Fats: 15.7g
Snack:
2 peaches
1 oz walnuts
Nutritional values: Kcal: 293 Protein: 9.6g, Carbs: 30.8g, Dietary Fiber: 6.5g, Fats: 17.5g
Lunch:
7 oz hummus
1 oz buckwheat bread
7 oz carrot sticks
Nutritional values: Kcal: 486 Protein: 19.5g, Carbs: 62.2g, Dietary Fiber: 17.5g, Fats: 20g
Snack:
3.5 oz cherries
Nutritional values: Kcal: 114 Protein: 0.4g, Carbs: 27.8g, Dietary Fiber: 0.6g, Fats: 0.1g
Dinner:
7 oz sweet potato, baked
¼ cup kidney beans, cooked
1 oz buckwheat bread
1 cup of herbal tea
Nutritional values: Kcal: 410 Protein: 16.5g, Carbs: 83.6g, Dietary Fiber: 14.3g, Fats: 1.8g

Day 11:
Breakfast
1 cup almond yogurt
7 oz pineapple chunks
1 large orange
1 cup of herbal tea
Nutritional values: Kcal: 362 Protein: 16.8g, Carbs: 65.4g, Dietary Fiber: 7.2g, Fats: 3.5g
Snack:
2 slices buckwheat bread
1 medium-sized tomato, fresh
1 small cucumber
1 red onion, fresh
1 tbsp olive oil
Nutritional values: Kcal: 268 Protein: 5.1g, Carbs: 32.7g, Dietary Fiber: 5g, Fats: 15.1g
Lunch:
3.5 oz enoki mushrooms, grilled
7 oz shiitake mushrooms, grilled
3.5 oz shishito peppers, grilled
2 oz buckwheat bread
Nutritional values: Kcal: 550 Protein: 20.6g, Carbs: 127g, Dietary Fiber: 34.3g, Fats: 5.8g
Snack:
7 oz cherries
Nutritional values: Kcal: 228 Protein: 0.7g, Carbs: 55.6g, Dietary Fiber: 1.2g, Fats: 0.1g
Dinner:
½ cup black beans, cooked
1 tbsp tahini
Nutritional values: Kcal: 420 Protein: 23.5g, Carbs: 63.7g, Dietary Fiber: 16.1g, Fats: 9.4g

Day 12:
Breakfast:
1 cup almond yogurt
1 tbsp chia seeds
3 figs
1 cup of black coffee
Nutritional values: Kcal: 457 Protein: 22.1g, Carbs: 64.2g, Dietary Fiber: 16g, Fats: 13.1g
Snack:
½ cup leek, cooked
1 medium-sized potato, cooked
½ cup shallots, cooked
1 tbsp olive oil
Nutritional values: Kcal: 369 Protein: 7g, Carbs: 56.9g, Dietary Fiber: 5.5g, Fats: 14.4g
Lunch:
1 cup edamame hummus
½ cup beets, cooked
½ cup shallots, fresh
Nutritional values: Kcal: 471 Protein: 36.6g, Carbs: 50.2g, Dietary Fiber: 12.4g, Fats: 17.6g
Snack:
1 cup of freshly squeezed lemon juice
1.5 oz walnuts
Nutritional values: Kcal: 321 Protein: 12.2g, Carbs: 9.3g, Dietary Fiber: 3.9g, Fats: 27g
Dinner:
10 oz mushrooms, grilled
½ cup basmati rice, cooked
Nutritional values: Kcal: 398 Protein: 15.5g, Carbs: 83.3g, Dietary Fiber: 4g, Fats: 1.4g

Day 13
Breakfast:
2 cups grapes
1 large orange
2 kiwis
1 cup lemonade
Nutritional values: Kcal: 319 Protein: 5.3g, Carbs: 80.9g, Dietary Fiber: 12.3g, Fats: 1.8g

Snack:
2 oz hazelnuts
Nutritional values: Kcal: 356 Protein: 8.5g, Carbs: 9.5g, Dietary Fiber: 5.5g, Fats: 34.5g

Lunch:
1 cup mushrooms, grilled
2 large carrots, grilled
1 medium-sized potato, cooked and mashed
1 red bell pepper, grilled
1 tbsp olive oil
Nutritional values: Kcal: 396 Protein: 8.9g, Carbs: 62.7g, Dietary Fiber: 10.5g, Fats: 14.7g

Snack:
2 medium apples
1 cup freshly squeezed orange juice
Nutritional values: Kcal: 344 Protein: 2.9g, Carbs: 87.4g, Dietary Fiber: 11.3g, Fats: 1.3g

Dinner:
3 oz red lentils, cooked
1 carrot cooked
7 oz kale, steamed
2 oz lettuce
Nutritional values: Kcal: 435 Protein: 28.7g, Carbs: 80.6g, Dietary Fiber: 31g, Fats: 1g

Day 14
Breakfast:
1 cup strawberries, fresh
¼ cup almond milk
1 medium apple
1 oz walnuts
Nutritional values: Kcal: 348 Protein: 4.8g, Carbs: 46g, Dietary Fiber: 10.1g, Fats: 19.7g

Snack:
4 large oranges, juiced
Nutritional values: Kcal: 272 Protein: 6.9g, Carbs: 86.4g, Dietary Fiber: 17.6g, Fats: 0.8g

Lunch:
½ cup barley, cooked
¼ cup red lentils, cooked
2 medium-sized tomatoes, fire-roasted
Nutritional values: Kcal: 539 Protein: 26g, Carbs: 106g, Dietary Fiber: 33.5g, Fats: 3.1g

Snack:
1 cup of freshly squeezed lemon juice
1.5 oz walnuts
Nutritional values: Kcal: 321 Protein: 12.2g, Carbs: 9.3g, Dietary Fiber: 3.9g, Fats: 27g

Dinner:
2 oz quinoa, cooked
2 oz white beans, cooked
7 oz spinach, sautéed
1 pear
Nutritional values: Kcal: 524 Protein: 27.4g, Carbs: 98.9g, Dietary Fiber: 21.3g, Fats: 4.9g

Day 15

Breakfast:
¼ cup rolled oats
¼ cup almond milk
1 oz brazil nuts
Nutritional values: Kcal: 401 Protein: 8.2g, Carbs: 20.6g, Dietary Fiber: 5.5g, Fats: 34.6g

Snack:
1 banana
1 oz pecan nuts
Nutritional values: Kcal: 302 Protein: 4.3g, Carbs: 31g, Dietary Fiber: 6.1g, Fats: 20.6g

Lunch:
7 oz artichoke, grilled
1 cup yellow wax beans, cooked
2 tbsp olive oil
2 oz lettuce
Nutritional values: Kcal: 375 Protein: 8.8g, Carbs: 30.4g, Dietary Fiber: 14.8g, Fats: 28.5g

Snack:
10 oz grapefruit
1 medium kiwi
1 oz walnuts
Nutritional values: Kcal: 312 Protein: 9.5g, Carbs: 36.9g, Dietary Fiber: 7.3g, Fats: 17.4g

Dinner:
½ cup green beans, cooked
1 medium-sized carrot, cooked
1 small sweet potato, cooked
½ cup broccoli, grilled
½ cup rice, cooked
Nutritional values: Kcal: 449 Protein: 10.6g, Carbs: 99.3g, Dietary Fiber: 7.8g, Fats: 0.9g

Day 16
Breakfast:
1 cup almond yogurt
2 oz prunes
1 tbsp flaxseed
1 tbsp pumpkin seeds
Nutritional values: Kcal: 394 Protein: 18.6g, Carbs: 57g, Dietary Fiber: 6.3g, Fats: 9.4g

Snack:
3.5 oz chestnuts, baked
1 medium-sized mango
Nutritional values: Kcal: 395 Protein: 4.4g, Carbs: 93.8g, Dietary Fiber: 5g, Fats: 2.5g

Lunch:
7 oz red bell peppers, grilled
1 tbsp olive oil
7 oz lettuce
1 cup freshly squeezed orange juice
Nutritional values: Kcal: 525 Protein: 11g, Carbs: 94.8g, Dietary Fiber: 13g, Fats: 17g

Snack:
½ medium-sized avocado
1 medium-sized tomato, fresh
2 slices buckwheat bread
1 large orange, juiced
Nutritional values: Kcal: 351 Protein: 5.6g, Carbs: 41.8g, Dietary Fiber: 12.3g, Fats: 25g

Dinner:
3.5 oz chickpeas, cooked
3.5 oz lettuce
7 oz zucchini, grilled
Nutritional values: Kcal: 406 Protein: 22g, Carbs: 69.8g, Dietary Fiber: 20.1g, Fats: 6.5g

Day 17
Breakfast:
3 Wasa crackers
½ cup almond yogurt
1 tbsp chia seeds
7 oz pomegranate seeds
Nutritional values: Kcal: 385 Protein: 14.7g, Carbs: 53.1g, Dietary Fiber: 11.8g, Fats: 11.1g
Snack:
4 cups blueberries, juiced
Nutritional values: Kcal: 280 Protein: 1.96g, Carbs: 85.8g, Dietary Fiber: 14.4g, Fats: 1.9g
Lunch:
1 medium-sized zucchini, grilled
2 large red bell peppers, grilled
1 tbsp olive oil
¼ cup basmati rice
1 fig
Nutritional values: Kcal: 405 Protein: 7.5g, Carbs: 64.7g, Dietary Fiber: 6.2g, Fats: 15.1g
Snack:
½ cup strawberries, blended
½ cup blueberries, blended
4 Graham crackers
Nutritional values: Kcal: 301 Protein: 4.9g, Carbs: 59g, Dietary Fiber: 4.8g, Fats: 6.1g
Dinner:
7 oz spinach, steamed
1 red onion, fresh
2 oz pine nuts
Nutritional values: Kcal: 471 Protein: 14.6g, Carbs: 24.9g, Dietary Fiber: 8.8g, Fats: 39.7g

Day 18
Breakfast
1 large apple, baked
1 cup of raspberries, fresh
1 oz pecan nuts
Nutritional values: Kcal: 377 Protein: 5.1g, Carbs: 49.5g, Dietary Fiber: 16.4g, Fats: 21.4g
Snack:
1 medium-sized grapefruit
1 oz walnuts
Nutritional values: Kcal: 216 Protein: 7.6g, Carbs: 13.2g, Dietary Fiber: 3.3g, Fats: 16.9g
Lunch:
½ cup brown rice, cooked
1 medium-sized carrot, cooked
¼ cup spring onions, fresh
Nutritional values: Kcal: 377 Protein: 8.1g, Carbs: 80.2g, Dietary Fiber: 5.4g, Fats: 2.6g
Snack:
2 Graham crackers
4 medium-sized apricots
10 oz raspberries
Nutritional values: Kcal: 333 Protein: 7.1g, Carbs: 70.7g, Dietary Fiber: 21.9g, Fats: 5.6g
Dinner:
3.5 oz green peas
7 oz spinach, stewed
1 oz almonds, toasted
2 tbsp olive oil
Nutritional values: Kcal: 530 Protein: 17.1g, Carbs: 27.6g, Dietary Fiber: 13g, Fats: 43.4g

Day 19
Breakfast
1 cup of blueberries, fresh
¼ cup of blackberries, fresh
5 walnuts
1 cup of herbal tea
Nutritional values: Kcal: 274 Protein: 8.3g, Carbs: 27.7g, Dietary Fiber: 7.3g, Fats: 17.2g
Snack:
1 cup edamame hummus
½ cup beets, cooked
½ cup shallots, fresh
Nutritional values: Kcal: 471 Protein: 36.6g, Carbs: 50.2g, Dietary Fiber: 12.4g, Fats: 17.6g
Lunch:
7 oz red bell peppers, grilled
1 tbsp olive oil
7 oz lettuce
1 cup freshly squeezed orange juice
Nutritional values: Kcal: 525 Protein: 11g, Carbs: 94.8g, Dietary Fiber: 13g, Fats: 17g
Snack:
1 medium-sized grapefruit
1 oz walnuts
Nutritional values: Kcal: 216 Protein: 7.6g, Carbs: 13.2g, Dietary Fiber: 3.3g, Fats: 16.9g
Dinner:
1 large zucchini, grilled and seasoned with 1 tbsp olive oil
2 slices buckwheat bread
1 pear
Nutritional values: Kcal: 403 Protein: 8.7g, Carbs: 60.7g, Dietary Fiber: 9.2g, Fats: 16.6g

Day 20
Breakfast:
1 cup of blueberries, fresh
¼ cup of blackberries, fresh
5 walnuts
1 cup of herbal tea
Nutritional values: Kcal: 274 Protein: 8.3g, Carbs: 27.7g, Dietary Fiber: 7.3g, Fats: 17.2g

Snack:
1 banana
1 oz pecan nuts
Nutritional values: Kcal: 302 Protein: 4.3g, Carbs: 31g, Dietary Fiber: 6.1g, Fats: 20.6g

Lunch:
1 medium-sized zucchini, grilled
2 large red bell peppers, grilled
1 tbsp olive oil
¼ cup basmati rice
1 fig
Nutritional values: Kcal: 405 Protein: 7.5g, Carbs: 64.7g, Dietary Fiber: 6.2g, Fats: 15.1g

Snack:
4 large oranges, juiced
Nutritional values: Kcal: 272 Protein: 6.9g, Carbs: 86.4g, Dietary Fiber: 17.6g, Fats: 0.8g

Dinner:
5 oz eggplant, steamed
½ cup red lentils, cooked
2 cherry tomatoes, fresh
Nutritional values: Kcal: 419 Protein: 28.3g, Carbs: 75.6g, Dietary Fiber: 37.2g, Fats: 1.8g

Day 21

Breakfast:
1 large baked apple
1 cup of freshly squeezed orange juice
Nutritional values: Kcal: 228 Protein: 2.3g, Carbs: 56.6g, Dietary Fiber: 5.9g, Fats: 0.9g

Snack:
10 oz honeydew melon, fresh
10 oz cherries, fresh
Nutritional values: Kcal: 428 Protein: 2.6g, Carbs: 105.1g, Dietary Fiber: 4g, Fats: 0.6g

Lunch:
5 oz arugula, fresh
½ cup white beans, cooked
1 red onion, fresh
Nutritional values: Kcal: 416 Protein: 28.5g, Carbs: 76.3g, Dietary Fiber: 20g, Fats: 1.9g

Snack:
1 medium-sized mango
4 medium-sized plums
Nutritional values: Kcal: 321 Protein: 4.8g, Carbs: 82g, Dietary Fiber: 8.6g, Fats: 2.1g

Dinner:
1 tomato, fire-roasted
1 zucchini, grilled
7 oz turnip greens, fresh
1 oz walnuts
1 cup freshly squeezed orange juice
Nutritional values: Kcal: 393 Protein: 14.4g, Carbs: 51.7g, Dietary Fiber: 11.7g, Fats: 18.3g

Day 22
Breakfast:
5 large strawberries
1 medium-sized apple
1 oz pecan nuts
1 cup of freshly squeezed orange juice
Nutritional values: Kcal: 454 Protein: 5.9g, Carbs: 67.6g, Dietary Fiber: 10.7g, Fats: 21.4g

Snack:
1 medium-sized grapefruit
1 oz walnuts
Nutritional values: Kcal: 216 Protein: 7.6g, Carbs: 13.2g, Dietary Fiber: 3.3g, Fats: 16.9g

Lunch:
1 tomato, fire-roasted
1 zucchini, grilled
7 oz turnip greens, fresh
1 oz walnuts
1 cup freshly squeezed orange juice
Nutritional values: Kcal: 393 Protein: 14.4g, Carbs: 51.7g, Dietary Fiber: 11.7g, Fats: 18.3g

Snack:
1 banana
1 oz pecan nuts
Nutritional values: Kcal: 302 Protein: 4.3g, Carbs: 31g, Dietary Fiber: 6.1g, Fats: 20.6g

Dinner:
10 oz shiitake mushrooms, grilled
4 oz leeks, stewed
3.5 oz radicchio, fresh
1 oz walnuts
Nutritional values: Kcal 420: Protein: 14.3g, Carbs: 62.4g, Dietary Fiber: 10.8g, Fats: 18g

Day23

Breakfast:

1 medium-sized guava
¼ cup rolled oats
¼ cup almond milk
1 oz almonds, toasted
Nutritional values: Kcal: 441 Protein: 12.4g, Carbs: 36.1g, Dietary Fiber: 11.8g, Fats: 30.7g

Snack:

1 cup of freshly squeezed lemon juice
1.5 oz walnuts
Nutritional values: Kcal: 321 Protein: 12.2g, Carbs: 9.3g, Dietary Fiber: 3.9g, Fats: 27g

Lunch:

1 cup cauliflower, cooked
1 cup edamame, cooked
Nutritional values: Kcal 401: Protein: 35.1g, Carbs: 33.6g, Dietary Fiber: 13.2g, Fats: 17.5g

Snack:

1 medium-sized mango
1 large orange, juiced
Nutritional values: Kcal: 287 Protein: 4.5g, Carbs: 71.6g, Dietary Fiber: 9.4g, Fats: 1.5g

Dinner:

5 oz ziti pasta
¼ cup green beans
Nutritional values: Kcal 417: Protein: 16.5g, Carbs: 79.5g, Dietary Fiber: 0.9g, Fats: 3.3g

Day 24
Breakfast:
1 whole wheat wrap
1 medium-sized tomato, fresh
4 oz avocado, fresh
½ cup spinach, steamed
Nutritional values: Kcal 428: Protein: 7.4g, Carbs: 45.3g, Dietary Fiber: 10.7g, Fats: 25.6g

Snack:
1 oz pecan nuts
Nutritional values: Kcal: 395 Protein: 6.1g, Carbs: 8.1g, Dietary Fiber: 6.1g, Fats: 40.5g

Lunch:
4 oz buckwheat spaghetti
2 oz cherry tomato
2 large plums
Nutritional values: Kcal 397: Protein: 13.8g, Carbs: 79.8g, Dietary Fiber: 2.4g, Fats: 3g

Snack:
10 oz grapefruit
1 medium-sized kiwi
Nutritional values: Kcal: 137 Protein: 2.7g, Carbs: 34g, Dietary Fiber: 5.4g, Fats: 0.7g

Dinner:
7 oz red bell peppers, grilled
1 tbsp olive oil
7 oz lettuce
1 cup freshly squeezed orange juice
Nutritional values: Kcal: 525 Protein: 11g, Carbs: 94.8g, Dietary Fiber: 13g, Fats: 17g

Day 25

Breakfast:
1 large apple, baked
1 cup of raspberries, fresh
1 cup of freshly squeezed orange juice
Nutritional values: Kcal: 292 Protein: 3.8g, Carbs: 71.3g, Dietary Fiber: 13.9g, Fats: 1.7g

Snack:
1 oz pecan nuts
Nutritional values: Kcal: 395 Protein: 6.1g, Carbs: 8.1g, Dietary Fiber: 6.1g, Fats: 40.5g

Lunch:
½ cup black beans, cooked
1 tbsp tahini
Nutritional values: Kcal: 420 Protein: 23.5g, Carbs: 63.7g, Dietary Fiber: 16.1g, Fats: 9.4g

Snack:
1 cup grapes
1 large mango
2 kiwis
Nutritional values: Kcal: 355 Protein: 5.1g, Carbs: 88.1g, Dietary Fiber: 10.4g, Fats: 2.4g

Dinner
10 oz Portobello mushrooms, grilled
½ cup basmati rice, cooked
Nutritional values: Kcal: 398 Protein: 15.5g, Carbs: 83.3g, Dietary Fiber: 4g, Fats: 1.4g

Day26

Breakfast:
2 bananas
1 tbsp pure coconut nectar
1 tbsp flaxseed
1 cup freshly squeezed lemonade
Nutritional values: Kcal: 369 Protein: 5.9g, Carbs: 78.3g, Dietary Fiber: 9.1g, Fats: 4.9g

Snack:
½ cup blueberries
1 oz almonds, toasted
1 oz walnuts
Nutritional values: Kcal: 381 Protein: 13.4g, Carbs: 19.4g, Dietary Fiber: 7.2g, Fats: 31.2g

Lunch:
2 medium-sized corn tortillas
¼ cup black beans, cooked
1 large tomato, diced
7 oz of spinach, steamed
1 medium-sized red bell pepper
Nutritional values: Kcal: 386 Protein: 21.7g, Carbs: 75g, Dietary Fiber: 18.5g, Fats: 3.5g

Snack:
1 peach
2 oz pecan nuts
Nutritional values: Kcal: 454 Protein: 7.5g, Carbs: 22.1g, Dietary Fiber: 8.4g, Fats: 40.9g

Dinner:
4 Roma tomatoes, grilled
½ cup rice, cooked
½ spinach, steamed
Nutritional values: Kcal: 436 Protein: 11.9g, Carbs: 92g, Dietary Fiber: 9.5g, Fats: 3.6g

Day 27
Breakfast:
2 cups grapes
1 large orange
2 kiwis
1 cup lemonade
Nutritional values: Kcal: 319 Protein: 5.3g, Carbs: 80.9g, Dietary Fiber: 12.3g, Fats: 1.8g
Snack:
1 oz pecan nuts
Nutritional values: Kcal: 395 Protein: 6.1g, Carbs: 8.1g, Dietary Fiber: 6.1g, Fats: 40.5g
Lunch:
2 medium-sized corn tortillas
¼ cup black beans, cooked
1 large tomato, diced
7 oz of spinach, steamed
1 medium-sized red bell pepper
Nutritional values: Kcal: 386 Protein: 21.7g, Carbs: 75g, Dietary Fiber: 18.5g, Fats: 3.5g
Snack:
10 oz honeydew melon, fresh
10 oz cherries, fresh
Nutritional values: Kcal: 428 Protein: 2.6g, Carbs: 105.1g, Dietary Fiber: 4g, Fats: 0.6g
Dinner:
5 oz eggplant, steamed
½ cup red lentils, cooked
2 cherry tomatoes, fresh
Nutritional values: Kcal: 419 Protein: 28.3g, Carbs: 75.6g, Dietary Fiber: 37.2g, Fats: 1.8g

Day 28

Breakfast:
10 oz avocado, baked
1 cup of herbal tea
Nutritional values: Kcal: 578 Protein: 5.4g, Carbs: 24.4g, Dietary Fiber: 19g, Fats: 55.3g

Snack:
1 medium-sized apple
Nutritional values: Kcal: 116 Protein: 0.6g, Carbs: 30.8g, Dietary Fiber: 5.4g, Fats: 0.4g

Lunch:
1 cup button mushrooms, grilled
2 large carrots, grilled
1 medium-sized potato, cooked and mashed
1 red bell pepper, grilled
1 tbsp olive oil
Nutritional values: Kcal: 396 Protein: 8.9g, Carbs: 62.7g, Dietary Fiber: 10.5g, Fats: 14.7g

Snack:
1 cup of freshly squeezed lemon juice
1.5 oz walnuts
Nutritional values: Kcal: 321 Protein: 12.2g, Carbs: 9.3g, Dietary Fiber: 3.9g, Fats: 27g

Dinner:
10 oz Portobello mushrooms, grilled
½ cup basmati rice, cooked
Nutritional values: Kcal: 398 Protein: 15.5g, Carbs: 83.3g, Dietary Fiber: 4g, Fats: 1.4g

Day 29
Breakfast:
1 cup almond yogurt
1 tbsp chia seeds
3 figs
1 cup of black coffee
Nutritional values: Kcal: 457 Protein: 22.1g, Carbs: 64.2g, Dietary Fiber: 16g, Fats: 13.1g
Snack:
1 oz pecan nuts
Nutritional values: Kcal: 395 Protein: 6.1g, Carbs: 8.1g, Dietary Fiber: 6.1g, Fats: 40.5g
Lunch:
½ cup brown rice, cooked
1 medium-sized carrot, cooked
¼ cup spring onions, fresh
Nutritional values: Kcal: 377 Protein: 8.1g, Carbs: 80.2g, Dietary Fiber: 5.4g, Fats: 2.6g
Snack:
1 banana
1 oz pecan nuts
Nutritional values: Kcal: 302 Protein: 4.3g, Carbs: 31g, Dietary Fiber: 6.1g, Fats: 20.6g
Dinner:
½ cup green beans, cooked
1 medium-sized carrot, cooked
1 small sweet potato, cooked
½ cup broccoli, grilled
½ cup rice, cooked
Nutritional values: Kcal: 449 Protein: 10.6g, Carbs: 99.3g, Dietary Fiber: 7.8g, Fats: 0.9g

Day 30
Breakfast:
1 large apple, baked
1 cup of raspberries, fresh
1 cup of freshly squeezed orange juice
Nutritional values: Kcal: 292 Protein: 3.8g, Carbs: 71.3g, Dietary Fiber: 13.9g, Fats: 1.7g

Snack:
10 oz honeydew melon, fresh
10 oz cherries, fresh
Nutritional values: Kcal: 428 Protein: 2.6g, Carbs: 105.1g, Dietary Fiber: 4g, Fats: 0.6g

Lunch:
3.5 oz buckwheat noodles, cooked and seasoned with one tablespoon of olive oil
2 oz spring onions, steamed
3.5 oz kale, steamed
Nutritional values: Kcal: 512 Protein: 16.1g, Carbs: 83.1g, Dietary Fiber: 12.7g, Fats: 17.2g

Snack:
10 oz grilled red peppers
10 oz melon
4 pecans
1 cup of herbal tea
Nutritional values: Kcal: 212 Protein: 7.7g, Carbs: 48.6g, Dietary Fiber: 6.8g, Fats: 1.8g

Dinner:
3 oz red lentils, cooked
1 carrot cooked
7 oz kale, steamed
2 oz lettuce
Nutritional values: Kcal: 435 Protein: 28.7g, Carbs: 80.6g, Dietary Fiber: 31g, Fats: 1g

Day 31
Breakfast:
1 cup of blueberries, fresh
¼ cup of blackberries, fresh
5 walnuts
1 cup of herbal tea
Nutritional values: Kcal: 274 Protein: 8.3g, Carbs: 27.7g, Dietary Fiber: 7.3g, Fats: 17.2g

Snack:
7 oz avocado, baked
Nutritional values: Kcal: 405 Protein: 3.8g, Carbs: 17.1g, Dietary Fiber: 13.3g, Fats: 38.7g

Lunch:
5 oz arugula, fresh
½ cup white beans, cooked
1 red onion, fresh
Nutritional values: Kcal: 416 Protein: 28.5g, Carbs: 76.3g, Dietary Fiber: 20g, Fats: 1.9g

Snack:
2 peaches
1 oz walnuts
Nutritional values: Kcal: 293 Protein: 9.6g, Carbs: 30.8g, Dietary Fiber: 6.5g, Fats: 17.5g

Dinner:
7 oz sweet potato, baked
¼ cup kidney beans, cooked
1 oz buckwheat bread
1 cup of herbal tea
Nutritional values: Kcal: 410 Protein: 16.5g, Carbs: 83.6g, Dietary Fiber: 14.3g, Fats: 1.8g

Day 32
Breakfast:
1 banana
4 oz cherries
1 buckwheat wrap
Nutritional values: Kcal: 406 Protein: 5.5g, Carbs: 88.9g, Dietary Fiber: 5g, Fats: 3.6g
Snack:
4 oz strawberries
4 Graham crackers
1 large orange, juiced
Nutritional values: Kcal: 360 Protein: 6.3g, Carbs: 73.3g, Dietary Fiber: 8.3g, Fats: 6.2g
Lunch:
½ cup button mushrooms, grilled
1 cup celery, fresh
½ cup black beans, cooked
1 peach
Nutritional values: Kcal: 413 Protein: 24.1g, Carbs: 78.6g, Dietary Fiber: 19g, Fats: 2g
Snack:
½ cup blueberries
1 oz almonds, toasted
1 oz walnuts
Nutritional values: Kcal: 381 Protein: 13.4g, Carbs: 19.4g, Dietary Fiber: 7.2g, Fats: 31.2g
Dinner:
½ small eggplant, grilled
½ cup kidney beans, cooked
2 oz raspberries
Nutritional values: Kcal: 397 Protein: 23.6g, Carbs: 76.6g, Dietary Fiber: 25.8g, Fats: 1.8g

Day 33

Breakfast:
1 banana
1 oz pecan nuts
Nutritional values: Kcal: 302 Protein: 4.3g, Carbs: 31g, Dietary Fiber: 6.1g, Fats: 20.6g

Snack:
2 oz almonds, toasted
1 medium-sized apple
Nutritional values: Kcal: 444 Protein: 12.6g, Carbs: 43g, Dietary Fiber: 12.5g, Fats: 28.8g

Lunch:
5 oz buckwheat noodles, cooked
2 oz tomato paste
1 small artichoke, steamed
4 dates
Nutritional values: Kcal: 396 Protein: 13.9g, Carbs: 84.7g, Dietary Fiber: 13.6g, Fats: 3.5g

Snack:
3.5 oz chestnuts, baked
1 medium-sized mango
Nutritional values: Kcal: 395 Protein: 4.4g, Carbs: 93.8g, Dietary Fiber: 5g, Fats: 2.5g

Dinner:
3 oz red lentils, cooked
1 carrot cooked
7 oz kale, steamed
2 oz lettuce
Nutritional values: Kcal: 435 Protein: 28.7g, Carbs: 80.6g, Dietary Fiber: 31g, Fats: 1g

Day 34
Breakfast:
1 cup of strawberries, fresh
½ cup raspberries, fresh
5 almonds, toasted
½ cup almond yogurt
1 cup of herbal tea
Nutritional values: Kcal: 200 Protein: 10g, Carbs: 28.3g, Dietary Fiber: 7.6g, Fats: 5.3g
Snack:
10 oz avocado, baked
1 cup of herbal tea
Nutritional values: Kcal: 578 Protein: 5.4g, Carbs: 24.4g, Dietary Fiber: 19g, Fats: 55.3g
Lunch:
½ cup brown rice, cooked
1 medium-sized carrot, cooked
¼ cup spring onions, fresh
Nutritional values: Kcal: 377 Protein: 8.1g, Carbs: 80.2g, Dietary Fiber: 5.4g, Fats: 2.6g
Snack:
1 medium-sized mango
4 medium-sized plums
Nutritional values: Kcal: 321 Protein: 4.8g, Carbs: 82g, Dietary Fiber: 8.6g, Fats: 2.1g
Dinner:
7 oz buckwheat noodles, cooked and seasoned with one tablespoon of olive oil
2 oz spring onions, steamed
Nutritional values: Kcal: 412 Protein: 10.1g, Carbs: 54.1g, Dietary Fiber: 3.8g, Fats: 18.2g

Day 35

Breakfast:
1 large baked apple
1 cup of freshly squeezed orange juice
Nutritional values: Kcal: 228 Protein: 2.3g, Carbs: 56.6g, Dietary Fiber: 5.9g, Fats: 0.9g

Snack:
3.5 oz walnuts
Nutritional values: Kcal: 613 Protein: 23.9g, Carbs: 9.8g, Dietary Fiber: 6.8g, Fats: 58.5g

Lunch:
5 oz shiitake mushrooms, grilled
1 white onion, grilled
1 tbsp olive oil
Nutritional values: Kcal: 241 Protein: 3.4g, Carbs: 29.8g, Dietary Fiber: 5.3g, Fats: 14.4g

Snack:
1 medium-sized grapefruit
1 oz walnuts
Nutritional values: Kcal: 257 Protein: 8.4g, Carbs: 23.5g, Dietary Fiber: 4.8g, Fats: 17g

Dinner:
7 oz sweet potato, baked
¼ cup kidney beans, cooked
1 oz buckwheat bread
1 cup of herbal tea
Nutritional values: Kcal: 410 Protein: 16.5g, Carbs: 83.6g, Dietary Fiber: 14.3g, Fats: 1.8g

Day 36
Breakfast:
2 bananas
1 tbsp pure coconut nectar
1 tbsp flaxseed
1 cup freshly squeezed lemonade
Nutritional values: Kcal: 369 Protein: 5.9g, Carbs: 78.3g, Dietary Fiber: 9.1g, Fats: 4.9g

Snack:
1 banana
1 oz pecan nuts
Nutritional values: Kcal: 302 Protein: 4.3g, Carbs: 31g, Dietary Fiber: 6.1g, Fats: 20.6g

Lunch:
1 cup edamame hummus
½ cup beets, cooked
½ cup shallots, fresh
Nutritional values: Kcal: 471 Protein: 36.6g, Carbs: 50.2g, Dietary Fiber: 12.4g, Fats: 17.6g

Snack:
7 oz chestnuts, baked
Nutritional values: Kcal: 389 Protein: 3.2g, Carbs: 87.7g, Dietary Fiber: 8.7g, Fats: 2.5g

Dinner:
1 tomato, fire-roasted
1 zucchini, grilled
7 oz turnip greens, fresh
1 oz walnuts
1 cup freshly squeezed orange juice
Nutritional values: Kcal: 393 Protein: 14.4g, Carbs: 51.7g, Dietary Fiber: 11.7g, Fats: 18.3g

Day 37
Breakfast:
1 large baked apple
1 cup of freshly squeezed orange juice
Nutritional values: Kcal: 228 Protein: 2.3g, Carbs: 56.6g, Dietary Fiber: 5.9g, Fats: 0.9g
Snack:
1 red bell pepper
1 yellow bell pepper
1 green bell pepper
1 cup avocado chunks
Nutritional values: Kcal: 412 Protein: 6.4g, Carbs: 39.6g, Dietary Fiber: 14.6g, Fats: 29.4g
Lunch:
2 cup butternut squash, cooked
1 cup brussel sprouts, cooked
1 cup leeks, cooked
1 tbsp olive oil
Nutritional values: Kcal: 338 Protein: 71g, Carbs: 53.3g, Dietary Fiber: 10.5g, Fats: 14.8g
Snack:
1 oz pecan nuts
Nutritional values: Kcal: 395 Protein: 6.1g, Carbs: 8.1g, Dietary Fiber: 6.1g, Fats: 40.5g
Dinner:
5 oz arugula, fresh
½ cup white beans, cooked
1 red onion, fresh
Nutritional values: Kcal: 416 Protein: 28.5g, Carbs: 76.3g, Dietary Fiber: 20g, Fats: 1.9g

Day 38

Breakfast:
2 apples, baked
1 cup of herbal tea
Nutritional values: Kcal: 234 Protein: 1.2g, Carbs: 62.1g, Dietary Fiber: 10.8g, Fats: 0.8g

Snack:
7 oz avocado, baked
Nutritional values: Kcal: 405 Protein: 3.8g, Carbs: 17.1g, Dietary Fiber: 13.3g, Fats: 38.7g

Lunch:
7 oz hummus
1 oz buckwheat bread
7 oz carrot sticks
Nutritional values: Kcal: 486 Protein: 19.5g, Carbs: 62.2g, Dietary Fiber: 17.5g, Fats: 20g

Snack:
1 medium-sized mango
4 medium-sized plums
Nutritional values: Kcal: 321 Protein: 4.8g, Carbs: 82g, Dietary Fiber: 8.6g, Fats: 2.1g

Dinner:
1 cup button mushrooms, grilled
2 large carrots, grilled
1 medium-sized potato, cooked and mashed
1 red bell pepper, grilled
1 tbsp olive oil
Nutritional values: Kcal: 396 Protein: 8.9g, Carbs: 62.7g, Dietary Fiber: 10.5g, Fats: 14.7g

Day 39

Breakfast:
1 large apple, baked
1 cup of raspberries, fresh
1 oz pecan nuts
Nutritional values: Kcal: 377 Protein: 5.1g, Carbs: 49.5g, Dietary Fiber: 16.4g, Fats: 21.4g

Snack:
1 avocado, juiced
Nutritional values: Kcal: 268 Protein: 4g, Carbs: 17.1g, Dietary Fiber: 13.5g, Fats: 29.4g

Lunch:
7 oz spinach, steamed
1 red onion, fresh
2 oz pine nuts
Nutritional values: Kcal: 471 Protein: 14.6g, Carbs: 24.9g, Dietary Fiber: 8.8g, Fats: 39.7g

Snack:
10 oz honeydew melon, fresh
10 oz cherries, fresh
Nutritional values: Kcal: 428 Protein: 2.6g, Carbs: 105.1g, Dietary Fiber: 4g, Fats: 0.6g

Dinner:
10 oz Portobello mushrooms, grilled
½ cup basmati rice, cooked
Nutritional values: Kcal: 398 Protein: 15.5g, Carbs: 83.3g, Dietary Fiber: 4g, Fats: 1.4g

Day 40
Breakfast:
1 large apple, baked
1 cup of raspberries, fresh
1 cup of freshly squeezed orange juice
Nutritional values: Kcal: 292 Protein: 3.8g, Carbs: 71.3g, Dietary Fiber: 13.9g, Fats: 1.7g

Snack:
1 peach
2 oz pecan nuts
Nutritional values: Kcal: 454 Protein: 7.5g, Carbs: 22.1g, Dietary Fiber: 8.4g, Fats: 40.9g

Lunch:
7 oz sweet potato, baked
¼ cup kidney beans, cooked
1 oz buckwheat bread
1 cup of herbal tea
Nutritional values: Kcal: 410 Protein: 16.5g, Carbs: 83.6g, Dietary Fiber: 14.3g, Fats: 1.8g

Snack:
1 kiwi
1.5 oz almonds, toasted
Nutritional values: Kcal: 292 Protein: 9.9g, Carbs: 20.2g, Dietary Fiber: 7.6g, Fats: 21.7g

Dinner:
10oz shiitake mushrooms, grilled
4 oz leeks, stewed
3.5 oz radicchio, fresh
1 oz walnuts
Nutritional values: Kcal 420: Protein: 14.3g, Carbs: 62.4g, Dietary Fiber: 10.8g, Fats: 18g

Day 41
Breakfast:
¼ cup rolled oats
¼ cup almond milk
1 oz brazil nuts
Nutritional values: Kcal: 401 Protein: 8.2g, Carbs: 20.6g, Dietary Fiber: 5.5g, Fats: 34.6g

Snack:
1 medium-sized mango
4 medium-sized plums
Nutritional values: Kcal: 321 Protein: 4.8g, Carbs: 82g, Dietary Fiber: 8.6g, Fats: 2.1g

Lunch:
3.5 oz green peas
7 oz spinach, stewed
1 oz almonds, toasted
2 tbsp olive oil
Nutritional values: Kcal: 530 Protein: 17.1g, Carbs: 27.6g, Dietary Fiber: 13g, Fats: 43.4g

Snack:
1 cup of freshly squeezed orange juice
Nutritional values: Kcal: 112 Protein: 1.7g, Carbs: 25.8g, Dietary Fiber: 0.5g, Fats: 0.5g

Dinner:
7 oz spinach, steamed
1 red onion, fresh
2 oz pine nuts
Nutritional values: Kcal: 471 Protein: 14.6g, Carbs: 24.9g, Dietary Fiber: 8.8g, Fats: 39.7g

Day 42

Breakfast
1 large apple, baked
1 cup of raspberries, fresh
1 cup of freshly squeezed orange juice
Nutritional values: Kcal: 292 Protein: 3.8g, Carbs: 71.3g, Dietary Fiber: 13.9g, Fats: 1.7g

Snack:
1 oz pecan nuts
Nutritional values: Kcal: 395 Protein: 6.1g, Carbs: 8.1g, Dietary Fiber: 6.1g, Fats: 40.5g

Lunch:
½ cup leek, cooked
1 medium-sized potato, cooked
½ cup shallots, cooked
1 tbsp olive oil
Nutritional values: Kcal: 369 Protein: 7g, Carbs: 56.9g, Dietary Fiber: 5.5g, Fats: 14.4g

Snack:
3.5 oz walnuts
Nutritional values: Kcal: 613 Protein: 23.9g, Carbs: 9.8g, Dietary Fiber: 6.8g, Fats: 58.5g

Dinner:
2 slices buckwheat bread
1 medium-sized tomato, fresh
1 small cucumber
1 red onion, fresh
1 tbsp olive oil
Nutritional values: Kcal: 268 Protein: 5.1g, Carbs: 32.7g, Dietary Fiber: 5g, Fats: 15.1g

Day 43

Breakfast
1 cup almond yogurt
7 oz pineapple chunks
1 large orange
1 cup of herbal tea
Nutritional values: Kcal: 362 Protein: 16.8g, Carbs: 65.4g, Dietary Fiber: 7.2g, Fats: 3.5g

Snack:
7 oz cherries
Nutritional values: Kcal: 228 Protein: 0.7g, Carbs: 55.6g, Dietary Fiber: 1.2g, Fats: 0.1g

Lunch:
½ cup barley, cooked
¼ cup red lentils, cooked
2 medium-sized tomatoes, fire-roasted
Nutritional values: Kcal: 539 Protein: 26g, Carbs: 106g, Dietary Fiber: 33.5g, Fats: 3.1g

Snack:
1 cup of freshly squeezed lemon juice
1.5 oz walnuts
Nutritional values: Kcal: 321 Protein: 12.2g, Carbs: 9.3g, Dietary Fiber: 3.9g, Fats: 27g

Dinner:
7 oz artichoke, grilled
1 cup yellow wax beans, cooked
2 tbsp olive oil
2 oz lettuce
Nutritional values: Kcal: 375 Protein: 8.8g, Carbs: 30.4g, Dietary Fiber: 14.8g, Fats: 28.5g

Day 44

Breakfast:
1 cup strawberries, fresh
¼ cup almond milk
1 medium-sized apple
1 oz walnuts
Nutritional values: Kcal: 348 Protein: 4.8g, Carbs: 46g, Dietary Fiber: 10.1g, Fats: 19.7g

Snack:
10 oz honeydew melon, fresh
10 oz cherries, fresh
Nutritional values: Kcal: 428 Protein: 2.6g, Carbs: 105.1g, Dietary Fiber: 4g, Fats: 0.6g

Lunch:
3.5 oz buckwheat pasta, cooked
1 large tomato
3.5 oz lettuce
Nutritional values: Kcal: 330 Protein: 13.2g, Carbs: 63.9g, Dietary Fiber: 2.7g, Fats: 2.8g

Snack:
10 oz grapefruit
1 medium-sized kiwi
1 oz walnuts
Nutritional values: Kcal: 312 Protein: 9.5g, Carbs: 36.9g, Dietary Fiber: 7.3g, Fats: 17.4g

Dinner:
7 oz buckwheat noodles, cooked and seasoned with one tablespoon of olive oil
2 oz spring onions, steamed
Nutritional values: Kcal: 412 Protein: 10.1g, Carbs: 54.1g, Dietary Fiber: 3.8g, Fats: 18.2g

Day 45

Breakfast:
1 cup almond yogurt
1 tbsp chia seeds
3 figs
1 cup of black coffee
Nutritional values: Kcal: 457 Protein: 22.1g, Carbs: 64.2g, Dietary Fiber: 16g, Fats: 13.1g

Snack:
4 cups blueberries, juiced
Nutritional values: Kcal: 280 Protein: 1.96g, Carbs: 85.8g, Dietary Fiber: 14.4g, Fats: 1.9g

Lunch:
7 oz artichoke
½ cup kidney beans
1 tbsp extra virgin olive oil
Nutritional values: Kcal: 523 Protein: 27.2g, Carbs: 77.2g, Dietary Fiber: 24.7g, Fats: 15.3g

Snack:
1 avocado, juiced
Nutritional values: Kcal: 268 Protein: 4g, Carbs: 17.1g, Dietary Fiber: 13.5g, Fats: 29.4g

Dinner:
7 oz arugula
1 cup raspberries
1 oz walnuts
1 cup freshly squeezed orange juice
Nutritional values: Kcal: 401 Protein: 15.1g, Carbs: 50.5g, Dietary Fiber: 13.6g, Fats: 19.3g

Day 46
Breakfast:
2 bananas
1 tbsp pure coconut nectar
1 tbsp flaxseed
1 cup freshly squeezed lemonade
Nutritional values: Kcal: 369 Protein: 5.9g, Carbs: 78.3g, Dietary Fiber: 9.1g, Fats: 4.9g

Snack:
1 cup of freshly squeezed lemon juice
1.5 oz walnuts
Nutritional values: Kcal: 321 Protein: 12.2g, Carbs: 9.3g, Dietary Fiber: 3.9g, Fats: 27g

Lunch:
5 oz eggplant, steamed
½ cup red lentils, cooked
2 cherry tomatoes, fresh
Nutritional values: Kcal: 419 Protein: 28.3g, Carbs: 75.6g, Dietary Fiber: 37.2g, Fats: 1.8g

Snack:
7 oz grapes
1 oz pecan nuts
Nutritional values: Kcal: 330 Protein: 4.3g, Carbs: 38.1g, Dietary Fiber: 4.8g, Fats: 20.9g

Dinner:
3 oz red lentils, cooked
1 carrot cooked
7 oz kale, steamed
2 oz lettuce
Nutritional values: Kcal: 435 Protein: 28.7g, Carbs: 80.6g, Dietary Fiber: 31g, Fats: 1g

Day 47
Breakfast:
½ cup quinoa, cooked
3 tbsp raisins
¼ cup coconut milk
1 cup of black coffee
Nutritional values: Kcal: 532 Protein: 14.2g, Carbs: 79.4g, Dietary Fiber: 8.3g, Fats: 19.6g

Snack:
1 cup cantaloupe, fresh
6 dates
Nutritional values: Kcal: 193 Protein: 2.5g, Carbs: 50.1g, Dietary Fiber: 5.4g, Fats: 0.5g

Lunch:
10oz shiitake mushrooms, grilled
4 oz leeks, stewed
3.5 oz radicchio, fresh
1 oz walnuts
Nutritional values: Kcal 420: Protein: 14.3g, Carbs: 62.4g, Dietary Fiber: 10.8g, Fats: 18g

Snack:
4 medium-sized apricots
10 oz raspberries
Nutritional values: Kcal: 214 Protein: 5.2g, Carbs: 49.2g, Dietary Fiber: 21.1g, Fats: 2.7g

Dinner:
4 Roma tomatoes, grilled
½ cup rice, cooked
½ spinach, steamed
Nutritional values: Kcal: 436 Protein: 11.9g, Carbs: 92g, Dietary Fiber: 9.5g, Fats: 3.6g

Day 48
Breakfast:
2 large oranges, broiled
2 oz walnuts
1 cup of herbal tea
Nutritional values: Kcal: 523 Protein: 17.1g, Carbs: 48.9g, Dietary Fiber: 12.7g, Fats: 33.9g
Snack:
1 avocado, juiced
Nutritional values: Kcal: 268 Protein: 4g, Carbs: 17.1g, Dietary Fiber: 13.5g, Fats: 29.4g
Lunch:
3.5 oz green peas
7 oz spinach, stewed
1 oz almonds, toasted
2 tbsp olive oil
Nutritional values: Kcal: 530 Protein: 17.1g, Carbs: 27.6g, Dietary Fiber: 13g, Fats: 43.4g
Snack:
1 medium-sized orange
Nutritional values: Kcal: 86 Protein: 1.7g, Carbs: 21.6g, Dietary Fiber: 4.4g, Fats: 0.2g
Dinner:
½ cup brown rice, cooked
1 medium-sized carrot, cooked
¼ cup spring onions, fresh
Nutritional values: Kcal: 377 Protein: 8.1g, Carbs: 80.2g, Dietary Fiber: 5.4g, Fats: 2.6g

Day 49

Breakfast:
1 large apple, baked
1 cup of raspberries, fresh
1 oz pecan nuts
Nutritional values: Kcal: 377 Protein: 5.1g, Carbs: 49.5g, Dietary Fiber: 16.4g, Fats: 21.4g

Snack:
2 Graham crackers
4 medium-sized apricots
10 oz raspberries
Nutritional values: Kcal: 333 Protein: 7.1g, Carbs: 70.7g, Dietary Fiber: 21.9g, Fats: 5.6g

Lunch:
1 medium-sized zucchini, grilled
2 large red bell peppers, grilled
1 tbsp olive oil
¼ cup basmati rice
1 fig
Nutritional values: Kcal: 405 Protein: 7.5g, Carbs: 64.7g, Dietary Fiber: 6.2g, Fats: 15.1g

Snack:
½ medium-sized avocado
1 medium-sized tomato, fresh
2 slices buckwheat bread
1 large orange, juiced
Nutritional values: Kcal: 351 Protein: 5.6g, Carbs: 41.8g, Dietary Fiber: 12.3g, Fats: 25g

Dinner
7 oz red bell peppers, grilled
1 tbsp olive oil
7 oz lettuce
1 cup freshly squeezed orange juice
Nutritional values: Kcal: 525 Protein: 11g, Carbs: 94.8g, Dietary Fiber: 13g, Fats: 17g

Day 50
Breakfast:
5 large strawberries
1 medium-sized apple
1 oz pecan nuts
1 cup of freshly squeezed orange juice
Nutritional values: Kcal: 454 Protein: 5.9g, Carbs: 67.6g, Dietary Fiber: 10.7g, Fats: 21.4g
Snack:
4 large oranges, juiced
Nutritional values: Kcal: 272 Protein: 6.9g, Carbs: 86.4g, Dietary Fiber: 17.6g, Fats: 0.8g
Lunch:
2 oz quinoa, cooked
2 oz white beans, cooked
7 oz spinach, sautéed
1 pear
Nutritional values: Kcal: 524 Protein: 27.4g, Carbs: 98.9g, Dietary Fiber: 21.3g, Fats: 4.9g
Snack:
3.5 oz cherries
Nutritional values: Kcal: 114 Protein: 0.4g, Carbs: 27.8g, Dietary Fiber: 0.6g, Fats: 0.1g
Dinner:
10 oz button mushrooms, grilled
4 oz leeks, stewed
3.5 oz radicchio, fresh
1 oz walnuts
Nutritional values: Kcal 420: Protein: 14.3g, Carbs: 62.4g, Dietary Fiber: 10.8g, Fats: 18g

Day 51
Breakfast:
¼ cup rolled oats
¼ cup almond milk
1 oz brazil nuts
Nutritional values: Kcal: 401 Protein: 8.2g, Carbs: 20.6g, Dietary Fiber: 5.5g, Fats: 34.6g

Snack:
10 oz grapefruit
1 medium-sized kiwi
1 oz walnuts
Nutritional values: Kcal: 312 Protein: 9.5g, Carbs: 36.9g, Dietary Fiber: 7.3g, Fats: 17.4g

Lunch:
½ cup green beans, cooked
1 medium-sized carrot, cooked
1 small sweet potato, cooked
½ cup broccoli, grilled
½ cup rice, cooked
Nutritional values: Kcal: 449 Protein: 10.6g, Carbs: 99.3g, Dietary Fiber: 7.8g, Fats: 0.9g

Snack:
1 medium-sized grapefruit
1 oz walnuts
Nutritional values: Kcal: 216 Protein: 7.6g, Carbs: 13.2g, Dietary Fiber: 3.3g, Fats: 16.9g

Dinner:
1 tomato, fire-roasted
1 zucchini, grilled
7 oz turnip greens, fresh
1 oz walnuts
1 cup freshly squeezed orange juice
Nutritional values: Kcal: 393 Protein: 14.4g, Carbs: 51.7g, Dietary Fiber: 11.7g, Fats: 18.3g

Day 52

Breakfast:
10 oz grilled red peppers
2 oz quinoa, cooked
10 oz melon
4 pecans
1 cup of herbal tea
Nutritional values: Kcal: 421 Protein: 15.7g, Carbs: 85g, Dietary Fiber: 10.8g, Fats: 5.2g

Snack:
4 medium-sized apricots
10 oz raspberries
Nutritional values: Kcal: 214 Protein: 5.2g, Carbs: 49.2g, Dietary Fiber: 21.1g, Fats: 2.7g

Lunch:
3.5 oz buckwheat noodles, cooked and seasoned with one tablespoon of olive oil
2 oz spring onions, steamed
3.5 oz kale, steamed
Nutritional values: Kcal: 512 Protein: 16.1g, Carbs: 83.1g, Dietary Fiber: 12.7g, Fats: 17.2g

Snack:
2 peaches
1 oz walnuts
Nutritional values: Kcal: 293 Protein: 9.6g, Carbs: 30.8g, Dietary Fiber: 6.5g, Fats: 17.5g

Dinner:
7 oz hummus
1 oz buckwheat bread
7 oz carrot sticks
Nutritional values: Kcal: 486 Protein: 19.5g, Carbs: 62.2g, Dietary Fiber: 17.5g, Fats: 20g

Day 53
Breakfast:
10 oz tomatoes, grilled
7 oz asparagus, grilled
1 cup of freshly squeezed orange juice
4 large figs
Nutritional values: Kcal: 392 Protein: 11.1g, Carbs: 93.1g, Dietary Fiber: 15.5g, Fats: 2g
Snack:
1 medium-sized grapefruit
1 oz walnuts
Nutritional values: Kcal: 216 Protein: 7.6g, Carbs: 13.2g, Dietary Fiber: 3.3g, Fats: 16.9g
Lunch:
7 oz sweet potato, baked
¼ cup kidney beans, cooked
1 oz buckwheat bread
1 cup of herbal tea
Nutritional values: Kcal: 410 Protein: 16.5g, Carbs: 83.6g, Dietary Fiber: 14.3g, Fats: 1.8g
Snack:
4 cups blueberries, juiced
Nutritional values: Kcal: 280 Protein: 1.96g, Carbs: 85.8g, Dietary Fiber: 14.4g, Fats: 1.9g
Dinner:
7 oz artichoke
½ cup kidney beans
1 tbsp extra virgin olive oil
Nutritional values: Kcal: 523 Protein: 27.2g, Carbs: 77.2g, Dietary Fiber: 24.7g, Fats: 15.3g

Day 54
Breakfast:
1 cup of blueberries, fresh
¼ cup of blackberries, fresh
5 walnuts
1 cup of herbal tea
Nutritional values: Kcal: 274 Protein: 8.3g, Carbs: 27.7g, Dietary Fiber: 7.3g, Fats: 17.2g

Snack:
3 cups pineapple chunks, juiced
1 large Red apple, juiced
Nutritional values: Kcal: 315 Protein: 3.5g, Carbs: 92g, Dietary Fiber: 12.7g, Fats: 0.9g

Lunch:
7 oz artichoke
½ cup kidney beans
1 tbsp extra virgin olive oil
Nutritional values: Kcal: 523 Protein: 27.2g, Carbs: 77.2g, Dietary Fiber: 24.7g, Fats: 15.3g

Snack:
1 medium-sized grapefruit
1 oz walnuts
Nutritional values: Kcal: 216 Protein: 7.6g, Carbs: 13.2g, Dietary Fiber: 3.3g, Fats: 16.9g

Dinner:
4 Roma tomatoes, grilled
½ cup rice, cooked
½ spinach, steamed
Nutritional values: Kcal: 436 Protein: 11.9g, Carbs: 92g, Dietary Fiber: 9.5g, Fats: 3.6g

Day 55

Breakfast:
10 oz tomatoes, grilled
7 oz asparagus, grilled
1 cup of freshly squeezed orange juice
4 large figs
Nutritional values: Kcal: 392 Protein: 11.1g, Carbs: 93.1g, Dietary Fiber: 15.5g, Fats: 2g

Snack:
4 cups blueberries, juiced
Nutritional values: Kcal: 280 Protein: 1.96g, Carbs: 85.8g, Dietary Fiber: 14.4g, Fats: 1.9g

Lunch:
3 oz red lentils, cooked
1 carrot cooked
7 oz kale, steamed
2 oz lettuce
Nutritional values: Kcal: 435 Protein: 28.7g, Carbs: 80.6g, Dietary Fiber: 31g, Fats: 1g

Snack:
½ cup blueberries
1 oz almonds, toasted
Nutritional values: Kcal: 247 Protein: 7.1g, Carbs: 27.1g, Dietary Fiber: 7g, Fats: 14.7g

Dinner:
5 oz eggplant, steamed
½ cup red lentils, cooked
2 cherry tomatoes, fresh
Nutritional values: Kcal: 419 Protein: 28.3g, Carbs: 75.6g, Dietary Fiber: 37.2g, Fats: 1.8g

Day 56

Breakfast:
½ cup quinoa, cooked
3 tbsp raisins
¼ cup coconut milk
1 cup of black coffee
Nutritional values: Kcal: 532 Protein: 14.2g, Carbs: 79.4g, Dietary Fiber: 8.3g, Fats: 19.6g

Snack:
1 cup cantaloupe, fresh
6 dates
Nutritional values: Kcal: 193 Protein: 2.5g, Carbs: 50.1g, Dietary Fiber: 5.4g, Fats: 0.5g

Lunch:
3.5 oz buckwheat pasta, cooked
1 large tomato
3.5 oz lettuce
Nutritional values: Kcal: 330 Protein: 13.2g, Carbs: 63.9g, Dietary Fiber: 2.7g, Fats: 2.8g

Snack:
4 medium-sized apricots
10 oz raspberries
Nutritional values: Kcal: 214 Protein: 5.2g, Carbs: 49.2g, Dietary Fiber: 21.1g, Fats: 2.7g

Dinner:
4 Roma tomatoes, grilled
½ cup rice, cooked
½ spinach, steamed
Nutritional values: Kcal: 436 Protein: 11.9g, Carbs: 92g, Dietary Fiber: 9.5g, Fats: 3.6g

Day 57

Breakfast:
½ cup rolled oats
1 tbsp flaxseed
½ cup coconut milk
Nutritional values: Kcal: 468 Protein: 9.4g, Carbs: 36.4g, Dietary Fiber: 8.7g, Fats: 33.5g

Snack:
3 cups pineapple chunks, juiced
1 large Red apple, juiced
Nutritional values: Kcal: 315 Protein: 3.5g, Carbs: 92g, Dietary Fiber: 12.7g, Fats: 0.9g

Lunch:
1 cup green peas, cooked
½ cup hummus
7 oz shiitake mushrooms, grilled
1.5 oz cauliflower, grilled
Nutritional values: Kcal: 392 Protein: 25.9g, Carbs: 50.6g, Dietary Fiber: 19.4g, Fats: 13.2g

Snack:
1 large apple
2 medium-sized carrots
2 oz prunes
Nutritional values: Kcal: 302 Protein: 2.8g, Carbs: 79g, Dietary Fiber: 12.4g, Fats: 0.6g

Dinner:
3 oz red lentils, cooked
1 carrot cooked
7 oz kale, steamed
2 oz lettuce
Nutritional values: Kcal: 435 Protein: 28.7g, Carbs: 80.6g, Dietary Fiber: 31g, Fats: 1g

Day 58
Breakfast:
10 oz grilled red peppers
10 oz melon
4 pecans
1 cup of herbal tea
Nutritional values: Kcal: 212 Protein: 7.7g, Carbs: 48.6g, Dietary Fiber: 6.8g, Fats: 1.8g
Snack:
3 oz sweet potato, cooked and mashed
1 tbsp maple syrup
1 cup almond yogurt
Nutritional values: Kcal: 303 Protein: 15.7g, Carbs: 48.3g, Dietary Fiber: 2.8g, Fats: 3.2g
Lunch:
3.5 oz green peas
7 oz spinach, stewed
1 oz almonds, toasted
2 tbsp olive oil
Nutritional values: Kcal: 530 Protein: 17.1g, Carbs: 27.6g, Dietary Fiber: 13g, Fats: 43.4g
Snack:
2 large apples, juiced
Nutritional values: Kcal: 258 Protein: 1.4g, Carbs: 73.1g, Dietary Fiber: 12g, Fats: 1g
Dinner:
1 cup button mushrooms, grilled
2 large carrots, grilled
1 medium-sized potato, cooked and mashed
1 red bell pepper, grilled
1 tbsp olive oil
Nutritional values: Kcal: 396 Protein: 8.9g, Carbs: 62.7g, Dietary Fiber: 10.5g, Fats: 14.7g

Day 59

Breakfast:
1 large baked apple
1 cup of freshly squeezed orange juice
Nutritional values: Kcal: 228 Protein: 2.3g, Carbs: 56.6g, Dietary Fiber: 5.9g, Fats: 0.9g

Snack:
½ cup leek, cooked
1 medium-sized potato, cooked
½ cup shallots, cooked
1 tbsp olive oil
Nutritional values: Kcal: 369 Protein: 7g, Carbs: 56.9g, Dietary Fiber: 5.5g, Fats: 14.4g

Lunch:
½ cup brown rice, cooked
1 medium-sized carrot, cooked
¼ cup spring onions, fresh
Nutritional values: Kcal: 377 Protein: 8.1g, Carbs: 80.2g, Dietary Fiber: 5.4g, Fats: 2.6g

Snack:
2 large red delicious apples, juiced
Nutritional values: Kcal: 258 Protein: 1.4g, Carbs: 73.1g, Dietary Fiber: 12g, Fats: 1g

Dinner:
7 oz red bell peppers, grilled
1 tbsp olive oil
7 oz lettuce
1 cup freshly squeezed orange juice
Nutritional values: Kcal: 525 Protein: 11g, Carbs: 94.8g, Dietary Fiber: 13g, Fats: 17g

Day 60
Breakfast:
10 oz grilled red peppers
10 oz melon
4 pecans
1 cup of herbal tea
Nutritional values: Kcal: 212 Protein: 7.7g, Carbs: 48.6g, Dietary Fiber: 6.8g, Fats: 1.8g
Snack:
2 oz walnuts
Nutritional values: Kcal: 350 Protein: 13.6g, Carbs: 5.6g, Dietary Fiber: 3.9g, Fats: 33.5g
Lunch:
10 oz button mushrooms, grilled
4 oz leeks, stewed
3.5 oz radicchio, fresh
1 oz walnuts
Nutritional values: Kcal 420: Protein: 14.3g, Carbs: 62.4g, Dietary Fiber: 10.8g, Fats: 18g
Snack:
1 oz pecan nuts
Nutritional values: Kcal: 395 Protein: 6.1g, Carbs: 8.1g, Dietary Fiber: 6.1g, Fats: 40.5g
Dinner:
7 oz sweet potato, baked
¼ cup kidney beans, cooked
1 oz buckwheat bread
1 cup of herbal tea
Nutritional values: Kcal: 410 Protein: 16.5g, Carbs: 83.6g, Dietary Fiber: 14.3g, Fats: 1.8g

Day 61:
Breakfast
1 cup almond yogurt
7 oz pineapple chunks
1 large orange
1 cup of herbal tea
Nutritional values: Kcal: 362 Protein: 16.8g, Carbs: 65.4g, Dietary Fiber: 7.2g, Fats: 3.5g
Snack:
2 slices buckwheat bread
1 medium-sized tomato, fresh
1 small cucumber
1 red onion, fresh
1 tbsp olive oil
Nutritional values: Kcal: 268 Protein: 5.1g, Carbs: 32.7g, Dietary Fiber: 5g, Fats: 15.1g
Lunch:
3.5 oz enoki mushrooms, grilled
7 oz shiitake mushrooms, grilled
3.5 oz shishito peppers, grilled
2 oz buckwheat bread
Nutritional values: Kcal: 550 Protein: 20.6g, Carbs: 127g, Dietary Fiber: 34.3g, Fats: 5.8g
Snack:
7 oz cherries
Nutritional values: Kcal: 228 Protein: 0.7g, Carbs: 55.6g, Dietary Fiber: 1.2g, Fats: 0.1g
Dinner:
½ cup black beans, cooked
1 tbsp tahini
Nutritional values: Kcal: 420 Protein: 23.5g, Carbs: 63.7g, Dietary Fiber: 16.1g, Fats: 9.4g

Day 62:
Breakfast:
1 cup almond yogurt
1 tbsp chia seeds
3 figs
1 cup of black coffee
Nutritional values: Kcal: 457 Protein: 22.1g, Carbs: 64.2g, Dietary Fiber: 16g, Fats: 13.1g

Snack:
½ cup leek, cooked
1 medium-sized potato, cooked
½ cup shallots, cooked
1 tbsp olive oil
Nutritional values: Kcal: 369 Protein: 7g, Carbs: 56.9g, Dietary Fiber: 5.5g, Fats: 14.4g

Lunch:
1 cup edamame hummus
½ cup beets, cooked
½ cup shallots, fresh
Nutritional values: Kcal: 471 Protein: 36.6g, Carbs: 50.2g, Dietary Fiber: 12.4g, Fats: 17.6g

Snack:
1 cup of freshly squeezed lemon juice
1.5 oz walnuts
Nutritional values: Kcal: 321 Protein: 12.2g, Carbs: 9.3g, Dietary Fiber: 3.9g, Fats: 27g

Dinner:
10 oz mushrooms, grilled
½ cup basmati rice, cooked
Nutritional values: Kcal: 398 Protein: 15.5g, Carbs: 83.3g, Dietary Fiber: 4g, Fats: 1.4g

Day 63
Breakfast:
2 cups grapes
1 large orange
2 kiwis
1 cup lemonade
Nutritional values: Kcal: 319 Protein: 5.3g, Carbs: 80.9g, Dietary Fiber: 12.3g, Fats: 1.8g
Snack:
2 oz hazelnuts
Nutritional values: Kcal: 356 Protein: 8.5g, Carbs: 9.5g, Dietary Fiber: 5.5g, Fats: 34.5g
Lunch:
1 cup mushrooms, grilled
2 large carrots, grilled
1 medium-sized potato, cooked and mashed
1 red bell pepper, grilled
1 tbsp olive oil
Nutritional values: Kcal: 396 Protein: 8.9g, Carbs: 62.7g, Dietary Fiber: 10.5g, Fats: 14.7g
Snack:
2 medium apples
1 cup freshly squeezed orange juice
Nutritional values: Kcal: 344 Protein: 2.9g, Carbs: 87.4g, Dietary Fiber: 11.3g, Fats: 1.3g
Dinner:
3 oz red lentils, cooked
1 carrot cooked
7 oz kale, steamed
2 oz lettuce
Nutritional values: Kcal: 435 Protein: 28.7g, Carbs: 80.6g, Dietary Fiber: 31g, Fats: 1g

Day 64
Breakfast:
1 cup strawberries, fresh
¼ cup almond milk
1 medium apple
1 oz walnuts
Nutritional values: Kcal: 348 Protein: 4.8g, Carbs: 46g, Dietary Fiber: 10.1g, Fats: 19.7g
Snack:
4 large oranges, juiced
Nutritional values: Kcal: 272 Protein: 6.9g, Carbs: 86.4g, Dietary Fiber: 17.6g, Fats: 0.8g
Lunch:
½ cup barley, cooked
¼ cup red lentils, cooked
2 medium-sized tomatoes, fire-roasted
Nutritional values: Kcal: 539 Protein: 26g, Carbs: 106g, Dietary Fiber: 33.5g, Fats: 3.1g
Snack:
1 cup of freshly squeezed lemon juice
1.5 oz walnuts
Nutritional values: Kcal: 321 Protein: 12.2g, Carbs: 9.3g, Dietary Fiber: 3.9g, Fats: 27g
Dinner:
2 oz quinoa, cooked
2 oz white beans, cooked
7 oz spinach, sautéed
1 pear
Nutritional values: Kcal: 524 Protein: 27.4g, Carbs: 98.9g, Dietary Fiber: 21.3g, Fats: 4.9g

Day 65
Breakfast:
¼ cup rolled oats
¼ cup almond milk
1 oz brazil nuts
Nutritional values: Kcal: 401 Protein: 8.2g, Carbs: 20.6g, Dietary Fiber: 5.5g, Fats: 34.6g

Snack:
1 banana
1 oz pecan nuts
Nutritional values: Kcal: 302 Protein: 4.3g, Carbs: 31g, Dietary Fiber: 6.1g, Fats: 20.6g

Lunch:
7 oz artichoke, grilled
1 cup yellow wax beans, cooked
2 tbsp olive oil
2 oz lettuce
Nutritional values: Kcal: 375 Protein: 8.8g, Carbs: 30.4g, Dietary Fiber: 14.8g, Fats: 28.5g

Snack:
10 oz grapefruit
1 medium kiwi
1 oz walnuts
Nutritional values: Kcal: 312 Protein: 9.5g, Carbs: 36.9g, Dietary Fiber: 7.3g, Fats: 17.4g

Dinner:
½ cup green beans, cooked
1 medium-sized carrot, cooked
1 small sweet potato, cooked
½ cup broccoli, grilled
½ cup rice, cooked
Nutritional values: Kcal: 449 Protein: 10.6g, Carbs: 99.3g, Dietary Fiber: 7.8g, Fats: 0.9g

Day 66

Breakfast:
1 cup almond yogurt
2 oz prunes
1 tbsp flaxseed
1 tbsp pumpkin seeds
Nutritional values: Kcal: 394 Protein: 18.6g, Carbs: 57g, Dietary Fiber: 6.3g, Fats: 9.4g

Snack:
3.5 oz chestnuts, baked
1 medium-sized mango
Nutritional values: Kcal: 395 Protein: 4.4g, Carbs: 93.8g, Dietary Fiber: 5g, Fats: 2.5g

Lunch:
7 oz red bell peppers, grilled
1 tbsp olive oil
7 oz lettuce
1 cup freshly squeezed orange juice
Nutritional values: Kcal: 525 Protein: 11g, Carbs: 94.8g, Dietary Fiber: 13g, Fats: 17g

Snack:
½ medium-sized avocado
1 medium-sized tomato, fresh
2 slices buckwheat bread
1 large orange, juiced
Nutritional values: Kcal: 351 Protein: 5.6g, Carbs: 41.8g, Dietary Fiber: 12.3g, Fats: 25g

Dinner:
3.5 oz chickpeas, cooked
3.5 oz lettuce
7 oz zucchini, grilled
Nutritional values: Kcal: 406 Protein: 22g, Carbs: 69.8g, Dietary Fiber: 20.1g, Fats: 6.5g

Day 67
Breakfast:
3 Wasa crackers
½ cup almond yogurt
1 tbsp chia seeds
7 oz pomegranate seeds
Nutritional values: Kcal: 385 Protein: 14.7g, Carbs: 53.1g, Dietary Fiber: 11.8g, Fats: 11.1g
Snack:
4 cups blueberries, juiced
Nutritional values: Kcal: 280 Protein: 1.96g, Carbs: 85.8g, Dietary Fiber: 14.4g, Fats: 1.9g
Lunch:
1 medium-sized zucchini, grilled
2 large red bell peppers, grilled
1 tbsp olive oil
¼ cup basmati rice
1 fig
Nutritional values: Kcal: 405 Protein: 7.5g, Carbs: 64.7g, Dietary Fiber: 6.2g, Fats: 15.1g
Snack:
½ cup strawberries, blended
½ cup blueberries, blended
4 Graham crackers
Nutritional values: Kcal: 301 Protein: 4.9g, Carbs: 59g, Dietary Fiber: 4.8g, Fats: 6.1g
Dinner:
7 oz spinach, steamed
1 red onion, fresh
2 oz pine nuts
Nutritional values: Kcal: 471 Protein: 14.6g, Carbs: 24.9g, Dietary Fiber: 8.8g, Fats: 39.7g

Day 68
Breakfast
1 large apple, baked
1 cup of raspberries, fresh
1 oz pecan nuts
Nutritional values: Kcal: 377 Protein: 5.1g, Carbs: 49.5g, Dietary Fiber: 16.4g, Fats: 21.4g
Snack:
1 medium-sized grapefruit
1 oz walnuts
Nutritional values: Kcal: 216 Protein: 7.6g, Carbs: 13.2g, Dietary Fiber: 3.3g, Fats: 16.9g
Lunch:
½ cup brown rice, cooked
1 medium-sized carrot, cooked
¼ cup spring onions, fresh
Nutritional values: Kcal: 377 Protein: 8.1g, Carbs: 80.2g, Dietary Fiber: 5.4g, Fats: 2.6g
Snack:
2 Graham crackers
4 medium-sized apricots
10 oz raspberries
Nutritional values: Kcal: 333 Protein: 7.1g, Carbs: 70.7g, Dietary Fiber: 21.9g, Fats: 5.6g
Dinner:
3.5 oz green peas
7 oz spinach, stewed
1 oz almonds, toasted
2 tbsp olive oil
Nutritional values: Kcal: 530 Protein: 17.1g, Carbs: 27.6g, Dietary Fiber: 13g, Fats: 43.4g

Day 69

Breakfast
1 cup of blueberries, fresh
¼ cup of blackberries, fresh
5 walnuts
1 cup of herbal tea
Nutritional values: Kcal: 274 Protein: 8.3g, Carbs: 27.7g, Dietary Fiber: 7.3g, Fats: 17.2g

Snack:
1 cup edamame hummus
½ cup beets, cooked
½ cup shallots, fresh
Nutritional values: Kcal: 471 Protein: 36.6g, Carbs: 50.2g, Dietary Fiber: 12.4g, Fats: 17.6g

Lunch:
7 oz red bell peppers, grilled
1 tbsp olive oil
7 oz lettuce
1 cup freshly squeezed orange juice
Nutritional values: Kcal: 525 Protein: 11g, Carbs: 94.8g, Dietary Fiber: 13g, Fats: 17g

Snack:
1 medium-sized grapefruit
1 oz walnuts
Nutritional values: Kcal: 216 Protein: 7.6g, Carbs: 13.2g, Dietary Fiber: 3.3g, Fats: 16.9g

Dinner:
1 large zucchini, grilled and seasoned with 1 tbsp olive oil
2 slices buckwheat bread
1 pear
Nutritional values: Kcal: 403 Protein: 8.7g, Carbs: 60.7g, Dietary Fiber: 9.2g, Fats: 16.6g

Day 70

Breakfast:
1 cup of blueberries, fresh
¼ cup of blackberries, fresh
5 walnuts
1 cup of herbal tea
Nutritional values: Kcal: 274 Protein: 8.3g, Carbs: 27.7g, Dietary Fiber: 7.3g, Fats: 17.2g

Snack:
1 banana
1 oz pecan nuts
Nutritional values: Kcal: 302 Protein: 4.3g, Carbs: 31g, Dietary Fiber: 6.1g, Fats: 20.6g

Lunch:
1 medium-sized zucchini, grilled
2 large red bell peppers, grilled
1 tbsp olive oil
¼ cup basmati rice
1 fig
Nutritional values: Kcal: 405 Protein: 7.5g, Carbs: 64.7g, Dietary Fiber: 6.2g, Fats: 15.1g

Snack:
4 large oranges, juiced
Nutritional values: Kcal: 272 Protein: 6.9g, Carbs: 86.4g, Dietary Fiber: 17.6g, Fats: 0.8g

Dinner:
5 oz eggplant, steamed
½ cup red lentils, cooked
2 cherry tomatoes, fresh
Nutritional values: Kcal: 419 Protein: 28.3g, Carbs: 75.6g, Dietary Fiber: 37.2g, Fats: 1.8g

Day 71

Breakfast:
1 cup of blueberries, fresh
¼ cup of blackberries, fresh
5 walnuts
1 cup of herbal tea
Nutritional values: Kcal: 274 Protein: 8.3g, Carbs: 27.7g, Dietary Fiber: 7.3g, Fats: 17.2g

Snack:
7 oz avocado, baked
Nutritional values: Kcal: 405 Protein: 3.8g, Carbs: 17.1g, Dietary Fiber: 13.3g, Fats: 38.7g

Lunch:
5 oz arugula, fresh
½ cup white beans, cooked
1 red onion, fresh
Nutritional values: Kcal: 416 Protein: 28.5g, Carbs: 76.3g, Dietary Fiber: 20g, Fats: 1.9g

Snack:
2 peaches
1 oz walnuts
Nutritional values: Kcal: 293 Protein: 9.6g, Carbs: 30.8g, Dietary Fiber: 6.5g, Fats: 17.5g

Dinner:
7 oz sweet potato, baked
¼ cup kidney beans, cooked
1 oz buckwheat bread
1 cup of herbal tea
Nutritional values: Kcal: 410 Protein: 16.5g, Carbs: 83.6g, Dietary Fiber: 14.3g, Fats: 1.8g

Day 72
Breakfast:
1 banana
4 oz cherries
1 buckwheat wrap
Nutritional values: Kcal: 406 Protein: 5.5g, Carbs: 88.9g, Dietary Fiber: 5g, Fats: 3.6g

Snack:
4 oz strawberries
4 Graham crackers
1 large orange, juiced
Nutritional values: Kcal: 360 Protein: 6.3g, Carbs: 73.3g, Dietary Fiber: 8.3g, Fats: 6.2g

Lunch:
½ cup button mushrooms, grilled
1 cup celery, fresh
½ cup black beans, cooked
1 peach
Nutritional values: Kcal: 413 Protein: 24.1g, Carbs: 78.6g, Dietary Fiber: 19g, Fats: 2g

Snack:
½ cup blueberries
1 oz almonds, toasted
1 oz walnuts
Nutritional values: Kcal: 381 Protein: 13.4g, Carbs: 19.4g, Dietary Fiber: 7.2g, Fats: 31.2g

Dinner:
½ small eggplant, grilled
½ cup kidney beans, cooked
2 oz raspberries
Nutritional values: Kcal: 397 Protein: 23.6g, Carbs: 76.6g, Dietary Fiber: 25.8g, Fats: 1.8g

Day 73
Breakfast:
1 banana
1 oz pecan nuts
Nutritional values: Kcal: 302 Protein: 4.3g, Carbs: 31g, Dietary Fiber: 6.1g, Fats: 20.6g
Snack:
2 oz almonds, toasted
1 medium-sized apple
Nutritional values: Kcal: 444 Protein: 12.6g, Carbs: 43g, Dietary Fiber: 12.5g, Fats: 28.8g
Lunch:
5 oz buckwheat noodles, cooked
2 oz tomato paste
1 small artichoke, steamed
4 dates
Nutritional values: Kcal: 396 Protein: 13.9g, Carbs: 84.7g, Dietary Fiber: 13.6g, Fats: 3.5g
Snack:
3.5 oz chestnuts, baked
1 medium-sized mango
Nutritional values: Kcal: 395 Protein: 4.4g, Carbs: 93.8g, Dietary Fiber: 5g, Fats: 2.5g
Dinner:
3 oz red lentils, cooked
1 carrot cooked
7 oz kale, steamed
2 oz lettuce
Nutritional values: Kcal: 435 Protein: 28.7g, Carbs: 80.6g, Dietary Fiber: 31g, Fats: 1g

Day 74

Breakfast:
1 cup of strawberries, fresh
½ cup raspberries, fresh
5 almonds, toasted
½ cup almond yogurt
1 cup of herbal tea
Nutritional values: Kcal: 200 Protein: 10g, Carbs: 28.3g, Dietary Fiber: 7.6g, Fats: 5.3g

Snack:
10 oz avocado, baked
1 cup of herbal tea
Nutritional values: Kcal: 578 Protein: 5.4g, Carbs: 24.4g, Dietary Fiber: 19g, Fats: 55.3g

Lunch:
½ cup brown rice, cooked
1 medium-sized carrot, cooked
¼ cup spring onions, fresh
Nutritional values: Kcal: 377 Protein: 8.1g, Carbs: 80.2g, Dietary Fiber: 5.4g, Fats: 2.6g

Snack:
1 medium-sized mango
4 medium-sized plums
Nutritional values: Kcal: 321 Protein: 4.8g, Carbs: 82g, Dietary Fiber: 8.6g, Fats: 2.1g

Dinner:
7 oz buckwheat noodles, cooked and seasoned with one tablespoon of olive oil
2 oz spring onions, steamed
Nutritional values: Kcal: 412 Protein: 10.1g, Carbs: 54.1g, Dietary Fiber: 3.8g, Fats: 18.2g

Day 75

Breakfast:
1 large baked apple
1 cup of freshly squeezed orange juice
Nutritional values: Kcal: 228 Protein: 2.3g, Carbs: 56.6g, Dietary Fiber: 5.9g, Fats: 0.9g

Snack:
3.5 oz walnuts
Nutritional values: Kcal: 613 Protein: 23.9g, Carbs: 9.8g, Dietary Fiber: 6.8g, Fats: 58.5g

Lunch:
5 oz shiitake mushrooms, grilled
1 white onion, grilled
1 tbsp olive oil
Nutritional values: Kcal: 241 Protein: 3.4g, Carbs: 29.8g, Dietary Fiber: 5.3g, Fats: 14.4g

Snack:
1 medium-sized grapefruit
1 oz walnuts
Nutritional values: Kcal: 257 Protein: 8.4g, Carbs: 23.5g, Dietary Fiber: 4.8g, Fats: 17g

Dinner:
7 oz sweet potato, baked
¼ cup kidney beans, cooked
1 oz buckwheat bread
1 cup of herbal tea
Nutritional values: Kcal: 410 Protein: 16.5g, Carbs: 83.6g, Dietary Fiber: 14.3g, Fats: 1.8g

Day 76
Breakfast:
2 bananas
1 tbsp pure coconut nectar
1 tbsp flaxseed
1 cup freshly squeezed lemonade
Nutritional values: Kcal: 369 Protein: 5.9g, Carbs: 78.3g, Dietary Fiber: 9.1g, Fats: 4.9g

Snack:
1 banana
1 oz pecan nuts
Nutritional values: Kcal: 302 Protein: 4.3g, Carbs: 31g, Dietary Fiber: 6.1g, Fats: 20.6g

Lunch:
1 cup edamame hummus
½ cup beets, cooked
½ cup shallots, fresh
Nutritional values: Kcal: 471 Protein: 36.6g, Carbs: 50.2g, Dietary Fiber: 12.4g, Fats: 17.6g

Snack:
7 oz chestnuts, baked
Nutritional values: Kcal: 389 Protein: 3.2g, Carbs: 87.7g, Dietary Fiber: 8.7g, Fats: 2.5g

Dinner:
1 tomato, fire-roasted
1 zucchini, grilled
7 oz turnip greens, fresh
1 oz walnuts
1 cup freshly squeezed orange juice
Nutritional values: Kcal: 393 Protein: 14.4g, Carbs: 51.7g, Dietary Fiber: 11.7g, Fats: 18.3g

Day 77

Breakfast:
1 large baked apple
1 cup of freshly squeezed orange juice
Nutritional values: Kcal: 228 Protein: 2.3g, Carbs: 56.6g, Dietary Fiber: 5.9g, Fats: 0.9g

Snack:
1 red bell pepper
1 yellow bell pepper
1 green bell pepper
1 cup avocado chunks
Nutritional values: Kcal: 412 Protein: 6.4g, Carbs: 39.6g, Dietary Fiber: 14.6g, Fats: 29.4g

Lunch:
2 cup butternut squash, cooked
1 cup brussel sprouts, cooked
1 cup leeks, cooked
1 tbsp olive oil
Nutritional values: Kcal: 338 Protein: 71g, Carbs: 53.3g, Dietary Fiber: 10.5g, Fats: 14.8g

Snack:
1 oz pecan nuts
Nutritional values: Kcal: 395 Protein: 6.1g, Carbs: 8.1g, Dietary Fiber: 6.1g, Fats: 40.5g

Dinner:
5 oz arugula, fresh
½ cup white beans, cooked
1 red onion, fresh
Nutritional values: Kcal: 416 Protein: 28.5g, Carbs: 76.3g, Dietary Fiber: 20g, Fats: 1.9g

Day 78

Breakfast:
2 apples, baked
1 cup of herbal tea
Nutritional values: Kcal: 234 Protein: 1.2g, Carbs: 62.1g, Dietary Fiber: 10.8g, Fats: 0.8g

Snack:
7 oz avocado, baked
Nutritional values: Kcal: 405 Protein: 3.8g, Carbs: 17.1g, Dietary Fiber: 13.3g, Fats: 38.7g

Lunch:
7 oz hummus
1 oz buckwheat bread
7 oz carrot sticks
Nutritional values: Kcal: 486 Protein: 19.5g, Carbs: 62.2g, Dietary Fiber: 17.5g, Fats: 20g

Snack:
1 medium-sized mango
4 medium-sized plums
Nutritional values: Kcal: 321 Protein: 4.8g, Carbs: 82g, Dietary Fiber: 8.6g, Fats: 2.1g

Dinner:
1 cup button mushrooms, grilled
2 large carrots, grilled
1 medium-sized potato, cooked and mashed
1 red bell pepper, grilled
1 tbsp olive oil
Nutritional values: Kcal: 396 Protein: 8.9g, Carbs: 62.7g, Dietary Fiber: 10.5g, Fats: 14.7g

Day 79
Breakfast:
1 large apple, baked
1 cup of raspberries, fresh
1 oz pecan nuts
Nutritional values: Kcal: 377 Protein: 5.1g, Carbs: 49.5g, Dietary Fiber: 16.4g, Fats: 21.4g
Snack:
1 avocado, juiced
Nutritional values: Kcal: 268 Protein: 4g, Carbs: 17.1g, Dietary Fiber: 13.5g, Fats: 29.4g
Lunch:
7 oz spinach, steamed
1 red onion, fresh
2 oz pine nuts
Nutritional values: Kcal: 471 Protein: 14.6g, Carbs: 24.9g, Dietary Fiber: 8.8g, Fats: 39.7g
Snack:
10 oz honeydew melon, fresh
10 oz cherries, fresh
Nutritional values: Kcal: 428 Protein: 2.6g, Carbs: 105.1g, Dietary Fiber: 4g, Fats: 0.6g
Dinner:
10 oz Portobello mushrooms, grilled
½ cup basmati rice, cooked
Nutritional values: Kcal: 398 Protein: 15.5g, Carbs: 83.3g, Dietary Fiber: 4g, Fats: 1.4g

Day 80
Breakfast:
1 large apple, baked
1 cup of raspberries, fresh
1 cup of freshly squeezed orange juice
Nutritional values: Kcal: 292 Protein: 3.8g, Carbs: 71.3g, Dietary Fiber: 13.9g, Fats: 1.7g

Snack:
1 peach
2 oz pecan nuts
Nutritional values: Kcal: 454 Protein: 7.5g, Carbs: 22.1g, Dietary Fiber: 8.4g, Fats: 40.9g

Lunch:
7 oz sweet potato, baked
¼ cup kidney beans, cooked
1 oz buckwheat bread
1 cup of herbal tea
Nutritional values: Kcal: 410 Protein: 16.5g, Carbs: 83.6g, Dietary Fiber: 14.3g, Fats: 1.8g

Snack:
1 kiwi
1.5 oz almonds, toasted
Nutritional values: Kcal: 292 Protein: 9.9g, Carbs: 20.2g, Dietary Fiber: 7.6g, Fats: 21.7g

Dinner:
10oz shiitake mushrooms, grilled
4 oz leeks, stewed
3.5 oz radicchio, fresh
1 oz walnuts
Nutritional values: Kcal 420: Protein: 14.3g, Carbs: 62.4g, Dietary Fiber: 10.8g, Fats: 18g

Day 81
Breakfast:
¼ cup rolled oats
¼ cup almond milk
1 oz brazil nuts
Nutritional values: Kcal: 401 Protein: 8.2g, Carbs: 20.6g, Dietary Fiber: 5.5g, Fats: 34.6g
Snack:
10 oz grapefruit
1 medium-sized kiwi
1 oz walnuts
Nutritional values: Kcal: 312 Protein: 9.5g, Carbs: 36.9g, Dietary Fiber: 7.3g, Fats: 17.4g
Lunch:
½ cup green beans, cooked
1 medium-sized carrot, cooked
1 small sweet potato, cooked
½ cup broccoli, grilled
½ cup rice, cooked
Nutritional values: Kcal: 449 Protein: 10.6g, Carbs: 99.3g, Dietary Fiber: 7.8g, Fats: 0.9g
Snack:
1 medium-sized grapefruit
1 oz walnuts
Nutritional values: Kcal: 216 Protein: 7.6g, Carbs: 13.2g, Dietary Fiber: 3.3g, Fats: 16.9g
Dinner:
1 tomato, fire-roasted
1 zucchini, grilled
7 oz turnip greens, fresh
1 oz walnuts
1 cup freshly squeezed orange juice
Nutritional values: Kcal: 393 Protein: 14.4g, Carbs: 51.7g, Dietary Fiber: 11.7g, Fats: 18.3g

Day 82

Breakfast:
10 oz grilled red peppers
2 oz quinoa, cooked
10 oz melon
4 pecans
1 cup of herbal tea
Nutritional values: Kcal: 421 Protein: 15.7g, Carbs: 85g, Dietary Fiber: 10.8g, Fats: 5.2g

Snack:
4 medium-sized apricots
10 oz raspberries
Nutritional values: Kcal: 214 Protein: 5.2g, Carbs: 49.2g, Dietary Fiber: 21.1g, Fats: 2.7g

Lunch:
3.5 oz buckwheat noodles, cooked and seasoned with one tablespoon of olive oil
2 oz spring onions, steamed
3.5 oz kale, steamed
Nutritional values: Kcal: 512 Protein: 16.1g, Carbs: 83.1g, Dietary Fiber: 12.7g, Fats: 17.2g

Snack:
2 peaches
1 oz walnuts
Nutritional values: Kcal: 293 Protein: 9.6g, Carbs: 30.8g, Dietary Fiber: 6.5g, Fats: 17.5g

Dinner:
7 oz hummus
1 oz buckwheat bread
7 oz carrot sticks
Nutritional values: Kcal: 486 Protein: 19.5g, Carbs: 62.2g, Dietary Fiber: 17.5g, Fats: 20g

Day 83
Breakfast:
10 oz tomatoes, grilled
7 oz asparagus, grilled
1 cup of freshly squeezed orange juice
4 large figs
Nutritional values: Kcal: 392 Protein: 11.1g, Carbs: 93.1g, Dietary Fiber: 15.5g, Fats: 2g
Snack:
1 medium-sized grapefruit
1 oz walnuts
Nutritional values: Kcal: 216 Protein: 7.6g, Carbs: 13.2g, Dietary Fiber: 3.3g, Fats: 16.9g
Lunch:
7 oz sweet potato, baked
¼ cup kidney beans, cooked
1 oz buckwheat bread
1 cup of herbal tea
Nutritional values: Kcal: 410 Protein: 16.5g, Carbs: 83.6g, Dietary Fiber: 14.3g, Fats: 1.8g
Snack:
4 cups blueberries, juiced
Nutritional values: Kcal: 280 Protein: 1.96g, Carbs: 85.8g, Dietary Fiber: 14.4g, Fats: 1.9g
Dinner:
7 oz artichoke
½ cup kidney beans
1 tbsp extra virgin olive oil
Nutritional values: Kcal: 523 Protein: 27.2g, Carbs: 77.2g, Dietary Fiber: 24.7g, Fats: 15.3g

Day 84
Breakfast:
1 cup of blueberries, fresh
¼ cup of blackberries, fresh
5 walnuts
1 cup of herbal tea
Nutritional values: Kcal: 274 Protein: 8.3g, Carbs: 27.7g, Dietary Fiber: 7.3g, Fats: 17.2g

Snack:
3 cups pineapple chunks, juiced
1 large Red apple, juiced
Nutritional values: Kcal: 315 Protein: 3.5g, Carbs: 92g, Dietary Fiber: 12.7g, Fats: 0.9g

Lunch:
7 oz artichoke
½ cup kidney beans
1 tbsp extra virgin olive oil
Nutritional values: Kcal: 523 Protein: 27.2g, Carbs: 77.2g, Dietary Fiber: 24.7g, Fats: 15.3g

Snack:
1 medium-sized grapefruit
1 oz walnuts
Nutritional values: Kcal: 216 Protein: 7.6g, Carbs: 13.2g, Dietary Fiber: 3.3g, Fats: 16.9g

Dinner:
4 Roma tomatoes, grilled
½ cup rice, cooked
½ spinach, steamed
Nutritional values: Kcal: 436 Protein: 11.9g, Carbs: 92g, Dietary Fiber: 9.5g, Fats: 3.6g

Day 85
Breakfast:
10 oz tomatoes, grilled
7 oz asparagus, grilled
1 cup of freshly squeezed orange juice
4 large figs
Nutritional values: Kcal: 392 Protein: 11.1g, Carbs: 93.1g, Dietary Fiber: 15.5g, Fats: 2g

Snack:
4 cups blueberries, juiced
Nutritional values: Kcal: 280 Protein: 1.96g, Carbs: 85.8g, Dietary Fiber: 14.4g, Fats: 1.9g

Lunch:
3 oz red lentils, cooked
1 carrot cooked
7 oz kale, steamed
2 oz lettuce
Nutritional values: Kcal: 435 Protein: 28.7g, Carbs: 80.6g, Dietary Fiber: 31g, Fats: 1g

Snack:
½ cup blueberries
1 oz almonds, toasted
Nutritional values: Kcal: 247 Protein: 7.1g, Carbs: 27.1g, Dietary Fiber: 7g, Fats: 14.7g

Dinner:
5 oz eggplant, steamed
½ cup red lentils, cooked
2 cherry tomatoes, fresh
Nutritional values: Kcal: 419 Protein: 28.3g, Carbs: 75.6g, Dietary Fiber: 37.2g, Fats: 1.8g

Day 86

Breakfast:
½ cup quinoa, cooked
3 tbsp raisins
¼ cup coconut milk
1 cup of black coffee
Nutritional values: Kcal: 532 Protein: 14.2g, Carbs: 79.4g, Dietary Fiber: 8.3g, Fats: 19.6g

Snack:
1 cup cantaloupe, fresh
6 dates
Nutritional values: Kcal: 193 Protein: 2.5g, Carbs: 50.1g, Dietary Fiber: 5.4g, Fats: 0.5g

Lunch:
3.5 oz buckwheat pasta, cooked
1 large tomato
3.5 oz lettuce
Nutritional values: Kcal: 330 Protein: 13.2g, Carbs: 63.9g, Dietary Fiber: 2.7g, Fats: 2.8g

Snack:
4 medium-sized apricots
10 oz raspberries
Nutritional values: Kcal: 214 Protein: 5.2g, Carbs: 49.2g, Dietary Fiber: 21.1g, Fats: 2.7g

Dinner:
4 Roma tomatoes, grilled
½ cup rice, cooked
½ spinach, steamed
Nutritional values: Kcal: 436 Protein: 11.9g, Carbs: 92g, Dietary Fiber: 9.5g, Fats: 3.6g

Day 87

Breakfast:
½ cup rolled oats
1 tbsp flaxseed
½ cup coconut milk
Nutritional values: Kcal: 468 Protein: 9.4g, Carbs: 36.4g, Dietary Fiber: 8.7g, Fats: 33.5g

Snack:
3 cups pineapple chunks, juiced
1 large Red apple, juiced
Nutritional values: Kcal: 315 Protein: 3.5g, Carbs: 92g, Dietary Fiber: 12.7g, Fats: 0.9g

Lunch:
1 cup green peas, cooked
½ cup hummus
7 oz shiitake mushrooms, grilled
1.5 oz cauliflower, grilled
Nutritional values: Kcal: 392 Protein: 25.9g, Carbs: 50.6g, Dietary Fiber: 19.4g, Fats: 13.2g

Snack:
1 large apple
2 medium-sized carrots
2 oz prunes
Nutritional values: Kcal: 302 Protein: 2.8g, Carbs: 79g, Dietary Fiber: 12.4g, Fats: 0.6g

Dinner:
3 oz red lentils, cooked
1 carrot cooked
7 oz kale, steamed
2 oz lettuce
Nutritional values: Kcal: 435 Protein: 28.7g, Carbs: 80.6g, Dietary Fiber: 31g, Fats: 1g

Day 88
Breakfast:
10 oz grilled red peppers
10 oz melon
4 pecans
1 cup of herbal tea
Nutritional values: Kcal: 212 Protein: 7.7g, Carbs: 48.6g, Dietary Fiber: 6.8g, Fats: 1.8g
Snack:
3 oz sweet potato, cooked and mashed
1 tbsp maple syrup
1 cup almond yogurt
Nutritional values: Kcal: 303 Protein: 15.7g, Carbs: 48.3g, Dietary Fiber: 2.8g, Fats: 3.2g
Lunch:
3.5 oz green peas
7 oz spinach, stewed
1 oz almonds, toasted
2 tbsp olive oil
Nutritional values: Kcal: 530 Protein: 17.1g, Carbs: 27.6g, Dietary Fiber: 13g, Fats: 43.4g
Snack:
2 large apples, juiced
Nutritional values: Kcal: 258 Protein: 1.4g, Carbs: 73.1g, Dietary Fiber: 12g, Fats: 1g
Dinner:
1 cup button mushrooms, grilled
2 large carrots, grilled
1 medium-sized potato, cooked and mashed
1 red bell pepper, grilled
1 tbsp olive oil
Nutritional values: Kcal: 396 Protein: 8.9g, Carbs: 62.7g, Dietary Fiber: 10.5g, Fats: 14.7g

Day 89

Breakfast:
1 large baked apple
1 cup of freshly squeezed orange juice
Nutritional values: Kcal: 228 Protein: 2.3g, Carbs: 56.6g, Dietary Fiber: 5.9g, Fats: 0.9g

Snack:
½ cup leek, cooked
1 medium-sized potato, cooked
½ cup shallots, cooked
1 tbsp olive oil
Nutritional values: Kcal: 369 Protein: 7g, Carbs: 56.9g, Dietary Fiber: 5.5g, Fats: 14.4g

Lunch:
½ cup brown rice, cooked
1 medium-sized carrot, cooked
¼ cup spring onions, fresh
Nutritional values: Kcal: 377 Protein: 8.1g, Carbs: 80.2g, Dietary Fiber: 5.4g, Fats: 2.6g

Snack:
2 large red delicious apples, juiced
Nutritional values: Kcal: 258 Protein: 1.4g, Carbs: 73.1g, Dietary Fiber: 12g, Fats: 1g

Dinner:
7 oz red bell peppers, grilled
1 tbsp olive oil
7 oz lettuce
1 cup freshly squeezed orange juice
Nutritional values: Kcal: 525 Protein: 11g, Carbs: 94.8g, Dietary Fiber: 13g, Fats: 17g

Day 90
Breakfast:
10 oz grilled red peppers
10 oz melon
4 pecans
1 cup of herbal tea
Nutritional values: Kcal: 212 Protein: 7.7g, Carbs: 48.6g, Dietary Fiber: 6.8g, Fats: 1.8g
Snack:
2 oz walnuts
Nutritional values: Kcal: 350 Protein: 13.6g, Carbs: 5.6g, Dietary Fiber: 3.9g, Fats: 33.5g
Lunch:
10 oz button mushrooms, grilled
4 oz leeks, stewed
3.5 oz radicchio, fresh
1 oz walnuts
Nutritional values: Kcal 420: Protein: 14.3g, Carbs: 62.4g, Dietary Fiber: 10.8g, Fats: 18g
Snack:
1 oz pecan nuts
Nutritional values: Kcal: 395 Protein: 6.1g, Carbs: 8.1g, Dietary Fiber: 6.1g, Fats: 40.5g
Dinner:
7 oz sweet potato, baked
¼ cup kidney beans, cooked
1 oz buckwheat bread
1 cup of herbal tea
Nutritional values: Kcal: 410 Protein: 16.5g, Carbs: 83.6g, Dietary Fiber: 14.3g, Fats: 1.8g

Day 91
Breakfast:
½ cup rolled oats
1 tbsp flaxseed
½ cup coconut milk
Nutritional values: Kcal: 468 Protein: 9.4g, Carbs: 36.4g, Dietary Fiber: 8.7g, Fats: 33.5g

Snack:
1 oz pecans
1 large orange
Nutritional values: Kcal: 284 Protein: 4.8g, Carbs: 25.7g, Dietary Fiber: 7.5g, Fats: 4.8g

Lunch:
1 large zucchini, grilled and seasoned with 1 tbsp olive oil
2 slices buckwheat bread
1 pear
Nutritional values: Kcal: 403 Protein: 8.7g, Carbs: 60.7g, Dietary Fiber: 9.2g, Fats: 16.6g

Snack:
3 cups pineapple chunks, juiced
1 large apple, juiced
Nutritional values: Kcal: 315 Protein: 3.5g, Carbs: 92g, Dietary Fiber: 12.7g, Fats: 0.9g

Dinner
10 oz mushrooms, grilled
½ cup basmati rice, cooked
Nutritional values: Kcal: 398 Protein: 15.5g, Carbs: 83.3g, Dietary Fiber: 4g, Fats: 1.4g

Day 92

Breakfast:
1 cup almond yogurt
1 tbsp chia seeds
3 figs
1 cup of black coffee
Nutritional values: Kcal: 457 Protein: 22.1g, Carbs: 64.2g, Dietary Fiber: 16g, Fats: 13.1g

Snack:
½ avocado, grilled
3 plums
Nutritional values: Kcal: 295 Protein: 3.4g, Carbs: 32.6g, Dietary Fiber: 9.4g, Fats: 20.2g

Lunch:
1 cup green peas, cooked
½ cup hummus
7 oz mushrooms, grilled
1.5 oz cauliflower, grilled
Nutritional values: Kcal: 392 Protein: 25.9g, Carbs: 50.6g, Dietary Fiber: 19.4g, Fats: 13.2g

Snack:
1 large apple
2 medium-sized carrots
2 oz prunes
Nutritional values: Kcal: 302 Protein: 2.8g, Carbs: 79g, Dietary Fiber: 12.4g, Fats: 0.6g

Dinner:
7 oz buckwheat noodles, cooked and seasoned with one tablespoon of olive oil
2 oz spring onions, steamed
Nutritional values: Kcal: 412 Protein: 10.1g, Carbs: 54.1g, Dietary Fiber: 3.8g, Fats: 18.2g

Day 93

Breakfast:
10 oz tomatoes, grilled
7 oz asparagus, grilled
1 cup of freshly squeezed orange juice
4 large figs
Nutritional values: Kcal: 392 Protein: 11.1g, Carbs: 93.1g, Dietary Fiber: 15.5g, Fats: 2g

Snack:
1 cup grapes
1 large mango
2 kiwis
Nutritional values: Kcal: 355 Protein: 5.1g, Carbs: 88.1g, Dietary Fiber: 10.4g, Fats: 2.4g

Lunch:
7 oz artichoke
½ cup kidney beans
1 tbsp extra virgin olive oil
Nutritional values: Kcal: 523 Protein: 27.2g, Carbs: 77.2g, Dietary Fiber: 24.7g, Fats: 15.3g

Snack:
1 large apple
Nutritional values: Kcal: 116 Protein: 0.6g, Carbs: 30.8g, Dietary Fiber: 5.4g, Fats: 0.4g

Dinner:
7 oz arugula
1 cup raspberries
1 oz walnuts
1 cup freshly squeezed orange juice
Nutritional values: Kcal: 401 Protein: 15.1g, Carbs: 50.5g, Dietary Fiber: 13.6g, Fats: 19.3g

Day 94
Breakfast:
2 bananas
1 tbsp pure coconut nectar
1 tbsp flaxseed
1 cup freshly squeezed lemonade
Nutritional values: Kcal: 369 Protein: 5.9g, Carbs: 78.3g, Dietary Fiber: 9.1g, Fats: 4.9g

Snack:
½ cup blueberries
1 oz almonds, toasted
1 oz walnuts
Nutritional values: Kcal: 381 Protein: 13.4g, Carbs: 19.4g, Dietary Fiber: 7.2g, Fats: 31.2g

Lunch:
3 oz red lentils, cooked
1 carrot cooked
7 oz kale, steamed
2 oz lettuce
Nutritional values: Kcal: 435 Protein: 28.7g, Carbs: 80.6g, Dietary Fiber: 31g, Fats: 1g

Snack:
3 cups honeydew melon, juiced
1 cup watermelon, diced
Nutritional values: Kcal: 203 Protein: 3.5g, Carbs: 55g, Dietary Fiber: 4.5g, Fats: 0.9g

Dinner:
5 oz eggplant, steamed
½ cup red lentils, cooked
2 cherry tomatoes, fresh
Nutritional values: Kcal: 419 Protein: 28.3g, Carbs: 75.6g, Dietary Fiber: 37.2g, Fats: 1.8g

Day 95:
Breakfast:
½ cup quinoa, cooked
3 tbsp raisins
¼ cup coconut milk
1 cup of black coffee
Nutritional values: Kcal: 532 Protein: 14.2g, Carbs: 79.4g, Dietary Fiber: 8.3g, Fats: 19.6g

Snack:
1 oz pecan nuts
Nutritional values: Kcal: 197 Protein: 3g, Carbs: 4g, Dietary Fiber: 3g, Fats: 20.2g

Lunch:
2 medium-sized corn tortillas
¼ cup black beans, cooked
1 large tomato, diced
7 oz of spinach, steamed
1 red bell pepper
Nutritional values: Kcal: 386 Protein: 21.7g, Carbs: 75g, Dietary Fiber: 18.5g, Fats: 3.5g

Snack:
1 cup cantaloupe
6 dates
Nutritional values: Kcal: 193 Protein: 2.5g, Carbs: 50.1g, Dietary Fiber: 5.4g, Fats: 0.5g

Dinner:
1 cup edamame hummus
½ cup beets, cooked
½ cup shallots, fresh
Nutritional values: Kcal: 471 Protein: 36.6g, Carbs: 50.2g, Dietary Fiber: 12.4g, Fats: 17.6g

Day 96:
Breakfast:
1 cup of strawberries, fresh
½ cup raspberries, fresh
5 almonds, toasted
½ cup almond yogurt
1 cup of herbal tea
Nutritional values: Kcal: 200 Protein: 10g, Carbs: 28.3g, Dietary Fiber: 7.6g, Fats: 5.3g

Snack:
1 peach
2 oz pecan nuts
Nutritional values: Kcal: 454 Protein: 7.5g, Carbs: 22.1g, Dietary Fiber: 8.4g, Fats: 40.9g

Lunch:
4 Roma tomatoes, grilled
½ cup rice, cooked
½ spinach, steamed
Nutritional values: Kcal: 436 Protein: 11.9g, Carbs: 92g, Dietary Fiber: 9.5g, Fats: 3.6g

Snack:
1 red bell pepper
1 yellow bell pepper
1 green bell pepper
1 cup avocado chunks
Nutritional values: Kcal: 412 Protein: 6.4g, Carbs: 39.6g, Dietary Fiber: 14.6g, Fats: 29.4g

Dinner:
3.5 oz buckwheat pasta, cooked
1 large tomato
3.5 oz lettuce
Nutritional values: Kcal: 330 Protein: 13.2g, Carbs: 63.9g, Dietary Fiber: 2.7g, Fats: 2.8g

Day 97:

Breakfast:
2 large oranges, broiled
2 oz walnuts
1 cup of herbal tea
Nutritional values: Kcal: 523 Protein: 17.1g, Carbs: 48.9g, Dietary Fiber: 12.7g, Fats: 33.9g

Snack:
4 medium-sized oranges, juiced
Nutritional values: Kcal: 200 Protein: 4.9g, Carbs: 64.5g, Dietary Fiber: 12.4g, Fats: 0.6g

Lunch:
2 cup butternut squash, cooked
1 cup Brussel sprouts, cooked
1 cup leeks, cooked
1 tbsp olive oil
Nutritional values: Kcal: 338 Protein: 71g, Carbs: 53.3g, Dietary Fiber: 10.5g, Fats: 14.8g

Snack:
7 oz chestnuts, baked
Nutritional values: Kcal: 389 Protein: 3.2g, Carbs: 87.7g, Dietary Fiber: 8.7g, Fats: 2.5g

Dinner:
5 oz orzo pasta, cooked
½ cup zucchini, grilled
Nutritional values: Kcal: 417 Protein: 16.7g, Carbs: 79.5g, Dietary Fiber: 0.6g, Fats: 3.4g

Day 98:
Breakfast:
10 oz grilled red peppers
10 oz melon
4 pecans
1 cup of herbal tea
Nutritional values: Kcal: 212 Protein: 7.7g, Carbs: 48.6g, Dietary Fiber: 6.8g, Fats: 1.8g

Snack:
1 oz pecan nuts
Nutritional values: Kcal: 395 Protein: 6.1g, Carbs: 8.1g, Dietary Fiber: 6.1g, Fats: 40.5g

Lunch:
5 oz mushrooms, grilled
1 white onion, grilled
1 tbsp olive oil
Nutritional values: Kcal: 241 Protein: 3.4g, Carbs: 29.8g, Dietary Fiber: 5.3g, Fats: 14.4g

Snack:
7 oz avocado, baked
Nutritional values: Kcal: 405 Protein: 3.8g, Carbs: 17.1g, Dietary Fiber: 13.3g, Fats: 38.7g

Dinner:
1 tomato, fire-roasted
1 zucchini, grilled
7 oz turnip greens, fresh
1 oz walnuts
1 cup freshly squeezed orange juice
Nutritional values: Kcal: 393 Protein: 14.4g, Carbs: 51.7g, Dietary Fiber: 11.7g, Fats: 18.3g

Day 99:
Breakfast:
10 oz grilled red peppers
2 oz quinoa, cooked
10 oz melon
4 pecans
1 cup of herbal tea
Nutritional values: Kcal: 421 Protein: 15.7g, Carbs: 85g, Dietary Fiber: 10.8g, Fats: 5.2g

Snack:
1 kiwi
1.5 oz almonds, toasted
Nutritional values: Kcal: 292 Protein: 9.9g, Carbs: 20.2g, Dietary Fiber: 7.6g, Fats: 21.7g

Lunch:
5 oz arugula, fresh
½ cup white beans, cooked
1 red onion, fresh
Nutritional values: Kcal: 416 Protein: 28.5g, Carbs: 76.3g, Dietary Fiber: 20g, Fats: 1.9g

Snack:
1 medium apple
1 banana
Nutritional values: Kcal: 221 Protein: 1.9g, Carbs: 57.8g, Dietary Fiber: 8.5g, Fats: 0.8g

Dinner:
3.5 oz buckwheat noodles, cooked and seasoned with one tablespoon of olive oil
2 oz spring onions, steamed
3.5 oz kale, steamed
Nutritional values: Kcal: 512 Protein: 16.1g, Carbs: 83.1g, Dietary Fiber: 12.7g, Fats: 17.2g

Day 100

Breakfast:
¼ cup rolled oats
¼ cup almond milk
5 oz cherries
Nutritional values: Kcal: 379 Protein: 4.6g, Carbs: 56.8g, Dietary Fiber: 4.2g, Fats: 15.7g

Snack:
2 peaches
1 oz walnuts
Nutritional values: Kcal: 293 Protein: 9.6g, Carbs: 30.8g, Dietary Fiber: 6.5g, Fats: 17.5g

Lunch:
7 oz hummus
1 oz buckwheat bread
7 oz carrot sticks
Nutritional values: Kcal: 486 Protein: 19.5g, Carbs: 62.2g, Dietary Fiber: 17.5g, Fats: 20g

Snack:
3.5 oz cherries
Nutritional values: Kcal: 114 Protein: 0.4g, Carbs: 27.8g, Dietary Fiber: 0.6g, Fats: 0.1g

Dinner:
7 oz sweet potato, baked
¼ cup kidney beans, cooked
1 oz buckwheat bread
1 cup of herbal tea
Nutritional values: Kcal: 410 Protein: 16.5g, Carbs: 83.6g, Dietary Fiber: 14.3g, Fats: 1.8g